Study Guide for
TRADING FOR
A LIVING

WILEY FINANCE EDITIONS

THE NEW SCIENCE OF TECHNICAL ANALYSIS
Thomas R. DeMark

TRADING FOR A LIVING
Dr. Alexander Elder

STUDY GUIDE FOR TRADING FOR A LIVING
Dr. Alexander Elder

THE NEW MONEY MANAGEMENT: A FRAMEWORK FOR ASSET ALLOCATION
Ralph Vince

TECHNICAL ANALYSIS IN THE OPTIONS MARKET
Richard Hexton

CHAOS FOR TRADERS: APPLYING EXPERT TECHNIQUES TO MAXIMIZE
YOUR PROFITS
Bill Williams

TRADING ON THE EDGE
Guido J. Deboeck

THE NEW TRADER
Tushar S. Chande and Stanley Kroll

POINT AND FIGURE CHARTING
Thomas J. Dorsey

INTERMARKET TECHNICAL ANALYSIS
John J. Murphy

TRADING APPLICATIONS OF JAPANESE CANDLESTICK CHARTING
Gary S. Wagner and Brad L. Matheny

CHAOS AND ORDER IN THE CAPITAL MARKETS
Edgar E. Peters

FRACTAL MARKET ANALYSIS: APPLYING CHAOS THEORY TO INVESTMENT
AND ECONOMICS
Edgar E. Peters

UNDERSTANDING SWAPS
John F. Marshall and Kenneth R. Kapner

GENETIC ALGORITHMS AND INVESTMENT STRATEGIES
Richard J. Bauer, Jr.

FORECASTING FINANCIAL AND ECONOMIC CYCLES
Michael P. Niemira and Philip A. Klein

THE MATHEMATICS OF MONEY MANAGEMENT
Ralph Vince

FORECASTING FINANCIAL MARKETS
Tony Plummer

Study Guide for
TRADING FOR
A LIVING

Psychology
Trading Tactics
Money Management

Dr. Alexander Elder
Director,
elder.com

WILEY

John Wiley & Sons, Inc.

Library of Congress Cataloging-in-Publication Data

Elder, Alexander
    Study Guide for Trading for a living : psychology, trading tactics, money management / Alexander Elder.
        p.   cm.
    Includes bibliographical references and index.
    ISBN 0-471-59225-0
    1. Stocks. 2. Futures. 3. Options (Futures)   I. Title.
HG4661.E43   1992
332.64'5 — dc20   92-35165

Printed in the United States of America

23 22 21

Preface

Experienced traders often seem to glide through the markets, easily swinging into and out of trades. Their trading appears effortless, like downhill skiing on TV. The illusion vanishes when you clamp on a pair of skis and discover the bumps on the slope. If you want to rise to the level of a serious trader, you have to work, study, and do your homework.

I wrote this *Study Guide* to help you grow and succeed as a trader. It is based on my years of experience as a trader and a teacher of traders. The more you study the markets and your reactions to them, the more likely you are to succeed.

Each question in this guide is referenced to a specific section in my book *Trading for a Living* (Wiley, 1993). You can benefit from this guide whether you have read the book or not; but if you become deeply involved in these questions, you will want to read the relevant chapters in *Trading for a Living.*

Trading is partly a science and partly an art — partly objective and partly subjective. This guide asks questions about trading and provides answers — but reasonable people may disagree with some of the answers. Let this guide challenge you to think about the markets.

All questions in this guide are grouped by topic — psychology, money management, technical indicators, and so on. Write down your answers and look for patterns of your strengths and weaknesses. You need to learn more about yourself and the markets — good traders always learn.

When you answer questions relating to charts, cover the charts with a sheet of paper and move that sheet slowly from left to right. The job of an analyst and trader becomes harder as he or she approaches the right edge of the chart. Try to simulate the uncertainty of the markets in working with this guide.

Brokerage house records show that most traders are male. For this reason, you'll find that I commonly use a masculine pronoun (he) in the cases throughout this book. Of course, no disrespect is intended to women traders. In my experience, the few women who do get involved in trading succeed more often than men.

I am grateful to two former employees for reviewing the manuscript and making many useful suggestions. Fred G. Schutzman, CMT, used to work as an analyst at Financial Trading Seminars, Inc., before he left to become the president of BFF Trading, a futures money management firm in New York. Fred works seven days a week analyzing markets and building a successful money management business — but he found time to answer and critique all the questions here.

Carol Keegan Kayne used to manage Financial Trading Seminars, Inc., before she became a full-time mom. She is a stickler for the English language, and no writing project is finished until Carol checks it for clarity and weeds out errors!

Thanks to my former professors and students at the University of Tartu (Estonia), Albert Einstein College of Medicine (New York), and Columbia University for providing many opportunities to teach and develop my educational style. Thanks to the clients of Financial Trading Seminars, Inc., in Asia, North and South America, Europe, Australia, and Africa.

I hope this guide helps you to sharpen your skills and to become a better, more confident trader.

New York   Dr. Alexander Elder
November 1992

Contents

PART TWO   Answers and Rating Scales

Study Guide for
TRADING FOR
A LIVING

Learning to Become
a Better Trader

All questions in this *Study Guide* have been designed to challenge you and test your ability to think as a trader. Each chapter tests your knowledge of a major market topic — psychology, charting, money management, and so on. All chapters correspond to the chapters and sections in *Trading for a Living* (Wiley, 1993).

Each chapter begins with a brief introduction. There is a grid for writing down your answers, so that you can work with this book several times. Discuss your answers with your friends — try to benefit from their experiences as well as from your own.

Begin working with each chapter by answering the first three questions and then looking up their answers. If you get two out of three right, proceed to the rest of the chapter. If you get only one answer right, stop and study the recommended materials before going any further. Take your time working with these tests — this is not a speed-reading course.

After you've answered all the questions in a chapter, look up the answers in the back of this book. For more information, each answer directs you to a section in *Trading for a Living*. The rating scales that follow the answers allow you to measure your progress. If you get high marks, proceed to the next chapter; if you get low marks, study the recommended literature and retake the test.

Be sure to analyze why you answered some questions right and others wrong. Successful traders think about every completed trade, whether they make or lose money. You must learn from your mistakes as well as from your successes.

PART ONE

Questions

Introduction

Most traders lose money in the markets, wash out, and are never heard from again. If you want to become a successful trader, you must beat the long odds against you. You must learn to think and act differently from the rest of the crowd.

This book offers you several unorthodox trading ideas. The aim of this Introduction is to pause at the beginning of the journey and to see whether you are in tune with some of the unconventional thinking about trading.

Begin by answering the first three questions in this Introduction. If you get fewer than two answers right, please review the recommended reading materials before going any further.

Questions	Trial 1	Trial 2	Trial 3	Trial 4	Trial 5
1					
2					
3					
4					
5					
6					
7					
8					
Correct answers					

Question 1

Which of the following methods of making trading decisions can serve traders well in the long run?
    I. Fundamental analysis
    II. Inside information
    III. Hunches and tips
    IV. Technical analysis

    A. I and II
    B. II and III
    C. I and IV
    D. III and IV

Question 2

Which of the following components is *not* essential for trading success?
    A. Trading psychology
    B. Analytic method
    C. Connections with market insiders
    D. Money management method

Question 3

The best approach to reading a book on trading is to
    A. test all the ideas that interest you on your own market data
    B. incorporate all the ideas in your work
    C. not trust what you read—why would anyone share good trading ideas?
    D. ask other traders whether the ideas in the book worked for them

Question 4

Which of the following is *not* a major cause of trading losses?
   A. Slippage
   B. Commissions
   C. Emotional trading
   D. Theft

Question 5

Trader Jim and Trader John take opposite sides of a trade. Both pay commissions, and both get hit with slippage. Trader Jim, the winner, collects $920, while Trader John, the loser, is out $1080. The result of this trade illustrates the fact that trading is a
   A. zero-sum game
   B. positive expectations game
   C. Random Walk
   D. minus-sum game

Question 6

You buy a contract (100 oz) of gold at $400/oz on $1000 margin. Your roundtrip commission is $25. Which of the following statements is *false*?
   A. Your commission is 2.5 percent of margin.
   B. You have to make at least 2.5 percent profit to avoid losing money.
   C. Your commission is 0.0625 percent of contract value.
   D. When you control $40,000, do not quibble about $25.

Question 7

You place an order to buy a contract of gold (100 oz) at $400/oz and get filled at $400.20. Gold declines to $398; you tell your broker to sell and get filled at 397.70. Your slippage on the trade is

A. $30
B. $50
C. $500
D. $1050

Question 8

In the trade described in Questions 6 and 7, assume that another trader sold gold short to you and covered when you got out of your long position, for a $200 gross profit. His slippage and commission were the same as yours. The total gain to the trading industry from your trade represents what percentage of the winner's $200 gross "gain"?

A. 25 percent
B. 50 percent
C. 75 percent
D. 100 percent

I

Individual Psychology

The battle for trading profits is won or lost inside your head. Your biggest and most dangerous challenge comes not from the floor traders, not from some well-capitalized trading group, and not from some high-powered analyst. Your biggest hurdle on the road to trading success is the person holding this book — you. If you can manage your emotions and use your intellect, trading profits will follow.

A professional trader is cool, calm, and collected. He knows what he'll do if the market goes up or down. When he is not sure about what to do, he stays out of the market and calmly analyzes it from the sidelines. He is in control of himself and, by extension, in control of his trading. If you feel giddy with joy when the market goes in your favor or freeze in fear when it goes against you, your trading account is doomed. No analytic method or trading system can help a trader whose mind is clouded by fear or greed.

Answer the first three questions in this chapter. If you get fewer than two of them right, stop and review the recommended reading materials. If you answer two or three questions correctly, please proceed to the rest of this chapter. Do not rush, avoid the clichés, take your time to think.

Questions	Trial 1	Trial 2	Trial 3	Trial 4	Trial 5
9					
10					
11					
12					
13					
14					
15					
16					
17					
18					
19					
20					
21					
22					
23					
24					
25					
26					
27					
28					
29					
30					
31					
32					
33					
34					
35					
Correct answers					

Question 9

A successful trader's attitude toward risk is usually one of
   A. avoiding risk
   B. thriving on risk
   C. enjoying risky situations, even though losses hurt
   D. measuring each risk before taking it

Question 10

The goal of a good trader is to
   A. become the best trader he can
   B. make more money than other traders
   C. buy things that will set him apart from other traders
   D. win the respect of family and friends

Question 11

A trader has lost 20 percent of his account. He would best be advised to
   A. subscribe to a newsletter with the best verified track record
   B. purchase a trading system with a history of profitability and low drawdowns
   C. stop trading until he has analyzed his worst trades and determined the cause of his losses
   D. continue to trade because the laws of probability favor an eventual turn in his favor

Question 12

Having a large trading account is desirable for all of the following reasons *except* that

A. you have a greater safety cushion and can afford to lose more
B. you can diversify among more markets
C. you can afford to trade multiple contracts and fine-tune your entry and exit
D. your expenses represent a smaller percentage of your account

Question 13

Which two of the following statements about commercially sold trading systems are most accurate?

I. An extensive track record provides confidence that a system will continue to perform well.
II. The fact that a system is sold by a prominent trader provides an extra margin of confidence.
III. Trading systems are designed to fit old data and they self-destruct when markets change.
IV. You can buy a system from a top analyst and lose money using it.

A. I and II
B. I and III
C. II and III
D. III and IV

Question 14

Which of the following analytic methods has worked spectacularly well at some point in the hands of a famous guru?

A. Volume analysis
B. Elliott Wave theory
C. Speedlines
D. All of the above

Question 15

Mastery of which of the following methods is essential for successful trading?
  A. Cycles analysis
  B. Market Profile
  C. Gann analysis
  D. None of the above

Question 16

Trading on the advice of a guru most often leads to which of the following results?
  I. Profits
  II. Psychological dependence
  III. Mastery of the markets
  IV. Loss of initiative

  A. I and II
  B. II and IV
  C. III and IV
  D. I and III

Question 17

Which of the following statements about gambling is *not* true?
  A. Gambling is a social diversion that exists in virtually all cultures.
  B. A skilled professional may gamble as a means of earning his livelihood.
  C. People become addicted to the excitement of gambling.
  D. Gambling allows a quick acquisition of riches.

Question 18

Which of the following is a key sign of a gambling attitude toward trading?
   I. the inability to resist the urge to trade
   II. feeling elated when trades go well and ashamed after losing
   III. always reversing losing positions
   IV. a string of trading losses

   A. I only
   B. I and II
   C. I, II, and III
   D. I, II, III, and IV

Question 19

A trader's account shows a steady loss of equity. Every successful trade is followed by more losses. He could benefit from all of the following *except*
   A. sticking to his system if it has been proven by historical testing
   B. keeping and analyzing charts made at entering and exiting every trade, with written reasons for entry and exit
   C. keeping a diary describing his feelings while entering and exiting every trade
   D. developing a new trading system

Question 20

Within a year, all of the following occur in the life of a trader: He receives three traffic tickets; he must pay a penalty for filing his taxes late; he receives two reprimands for tardiness on his non-trading job; and his trading account is down 35 percent. Which of the following is the best advice for this trader?

A. It is a hard life. Try to make a lot of money trading, quit your job, and hire someone to handle your finances.
B. Traffic tickets have nothing to do with trading—don't worry about them.
C. You are sabotaging yourself and need to work on changing yourself as a person.
D. Hang in there; it is hard to keep a job and trade at the same time.

Question 21

Pick two correct statements about trading psychology.
   I. Your feelings have an immediate impact on your equity.
   II. To win you have to be more intelligent than most traders.
   III. Feeling high after profitable trades reinforces good trading habits.
   IV. Fear and greed have a greater impact on your equity than a brilliant trading system.

A. I and II
B. II and III
C. III and IV
D. I and IV

Question 22

You've made a series of successful trades over several months. Now is the time to
   I. congratulate yourself and increase the size of your positions
   II. use fewer stops
   III. take a vacation
   IV. realize that you have become a competent trader and can spend less time studying the markets

A. I and II
B. II and IV
C. I and III
D. III and IV

Question 23

The main goal of a person who is a member of Alcoholics Anonymous, from whom a trader may learn, is to
A. control the bad effects of drinking
B. go to sleep sober each day
C. not drink on workdays
D. find out what drives him to drink

Question 24

Losing traders often think and talk like drunks. An alcoholic says, "My boss fired me 'cause I was a few minutes late. My landlord is trying to evict me 'cause I'm a little late on my rent. I've gotta cut down on my drinking for a while and straighten it all out." This shows he is
A. managing his life
B. handling his problem realistically
C. trying to control the side effects of drinking
D. practicing denial

Question 25

Losers and alcoholics have a lot in common. The differences between an alcoholic and a social drinker include all of the following *except* that
A. a social drinker can stop after having one drink
B. an alcoholic keeps getting drunk until his life deteriorates

C. a social drinker decides when to drink and when to stop

D. a person who does not drink on workdays is not an alcoholic

Question 26

Losers and alcoholics share many traits. All of the following apply to alcoholics *except* that

A. if an alcoholic can stay sober for a year, he is safe to start drinking socially, in moderation

B. the first step toward recovery is the admission that one is powerless over alcohol

C. do not plan for the long term, stay sober one day at a time

D. the sooner an alcoholic has a crisis and hits "rock bottom," the better off he is

Question 27

The basic similarity between a losing trader and an alcoholic is:

A. Losers are addicted to the excitement of trading the way alcoholics are addicted to alcohol.

B. Losers hide the extent of their losses from themselves and others, just as alcoholics hide how much they drink.

C. Losers try to trade their way out of the hole, just as alcoholics try to switch from liquor to wine.

D. All of the above

Question 28

The psychology of losers involves all of the following *except* that

A. losers find trading very exciting, even when it leads to losses

B. few losers recover after they destroy their accounts

C. losers know that they have a personal problem with trading

D. losers usually shoot for a "big win"

Question 29

The first step in a bad trader's recovery from being a loser is to say,
   A. "I need a better trading system."
   B. "I must find a major bull market."
   C. "I need to learn new trading methods."
   D. "I am a loser."

Question 30

When a trader says, "My name is so-and-so and I am a loser" the result is
   I. a fearful attitude toward trading
   II. cutting losses short
   III. avoidance of overtrading
   IV. lower commissions and slippage

   A. I and II
   B. II and III
   C. III and IV
   D. I and IV

Question 31

The most important factor in becoming a successful trader is
   A. starting with a good-sized trading capital
   B. being able to learn from other successful traders
   C. using your intellect rather than making emotional decisions
   D. relying on useful skills in your business or professional background

Question 32

Most traders approach the markets in order to
    I. make money
    II. become independent
    III. take the challenge
    IV. be entertained

    A. I
    B. I and II
    C. I, II, and III
    D. I, II, III, and IV

Question 33

If the markets seem mysterious to you after a year of trading, it is because
    A. your trading behavior is unpredictable
    B. you lack good fundamental or technical information
    C. your account is too small
    D. the markets are chaotic (Random Walk)

Question 34

All of the following can help traders succeed in the long run *except*
    A. sticking to a money management plan
    B. using a tested system for finding trades
    C. stopping your trading to reflect after a series of losses
    D. removing the bulk of profits from your account

Question 35

A trade begins when
    A. The market appears overbought or oversold
    B. An indicator gives you an entry signal
    C. You decide to place a buy or sell order
    D. A newsletter makes an attractive recommendation

II

Mass Psychology

When you go long or short in the financial markets, you join a huge crowd of traders. They buy and sell, trying to profit from their opinions about future prices. Their fear and greed create huge waves of mass optimism and pessimism. These psychological tides, as strong as the tides in the ocean, sweep the markets, causing them to rise or fall. Crowds are big and strong — it is expensive to argue with them.

Crowds are strong but primitive. Their actions follow fairly simple laws of social psychology. Knowing those laws can help you run with the crowd when it is profitable and part ways when you see that a trend is about to end. The job of a market analyst is hard because crowds tend to suck us in even as we observe them. Anyone who has attended a political rally or a mass concert has felt the pull of the crowd.

Some questions in this chapter test your knowledge of the basic laws of crowd psychology as applied to the financial markets. Others help you test the impact of the trading crowd on your feelings and judgment.

Answer the first three questions in this chapter. If you get fewer than two answers right, please review the recommended reading materials. If you answer two or three questions correctly, proceed to the rest of this chapter.

Now is a good time to reflect on your feelings and actions, rational or irrational, when you trade. Try to relate your answers to these questions to your trading experiences.

Questions	Trial 1	Trial 2	Trial 3	Trial 4	Trial 5
36					
37					
38					
39					
40					
41					
42					
43					
44					
45					
46					
47					
48					
49					
50					
51					
52					
53					
54					
55					
Correct answers					

Question 36

Price is
  A. the intersection of supply and demand curves
  B. the value of a trading vehicle
  C. a reflection of company assets in the stock market; a reflection of demand for a commodity
  D. the consensus of value of all market participants at the moment of the trade

Question 37

Which of the following statements is *incorrect?*
  A. Bulls bet that prices will rise; they try to buy as low as possible.
  B. Undecided traders put pressure on bulls and bears by their mere presence.
  C. Bears bet that prices will fall; they want to sell as high as possible.
  D. The goal of a technical analyst is to forecast whether bulls or bears will win and whether prices will rise or fall.

Question 38

It will help you to understand what happens in the market if you think of the marketplace as a
  A. number of rational individuals acting to maximize their gains
  B. crowd whose members try to pick each other's pockets while being swayed by waves of greed and fear
  C. constant flow of data—a mix of useful information and chaos
  D. carnival packed with drunks offering money to strangers

Question 39

When you are not sure whether to buy or sell, it pays to
  A. stay away from the market or close out your positions
  B. seek advice from a currently "hot" guru
  C. watch financial news on TV or read a newspaper to find out what others are doing
  D. trade a smaller size than usual

Question 40

Any profits you make in trading come from
  A. the brokers
  B. the economy
  C. the traders
  D. the exchanges

Question 41

Trading on inside information
  I. is criminal in the United States
  II. is legal overseas
  III. can lead to losses
  IV. is legal in the futures markets

  A. I
  B. I and II
  C. I, II, and III
  D. I, II, III, and IV

Question 42

Institutional traders have all these advantages over private traders *except*
   A. deep pockets
   B. inside information
   C. greater flexibility
   D. better training

Question 43

Private traders
   I. usually come to the market after a successful career
   II. usually lose money trading
   III. often trade for the challenge or for the thrill
   IV. have no discipline imposed on them

   A. I
   B. I and II
   C. I, II, and III
   D. I, II, III, and IV

Question 44

Advisory newsletters
   I. can help you learn new trading ideas
   II. can provide good entertainment
   III. are written by trading experts
   IV. offer a good way to make money in the markets

A. I and II
B. II and III
C. III and IV
D. I and IV

Question 45

When a person joins a crowd, he
  I. becomes more impulsive and emotional
  II. benefits from the strengths of others
  III. trusts crowd members and leaders more than himself
  IV. can leave the crowd when he wants to

A. I and II
B. I and III
C. II and III
D. II and IV

Question 46

People join crowds out of a
  I. fear of uncertainty
  II. lifelong habit
  III. desire to be led by strong leaders
  IV. search for comfort

A. I
B. I and II
C. I, II, and III
D. I, II, III, and IV

Question 47

Which of these statements are true?
 I. Crowds are primitive; it is OK to use simple trading strategies.
 II. You can bet against the market and win.
 III. A good trader feels elated when the market goes in his direction
      and depressed when it goes against him.
 IV. Market crowds are almost always wrong.

A. I
B. I and II
C. I, II, and III
D. I, II, III, and IV

Question 48

Identify the main leader of market trends.
 A. Powerful financial interests
 B. Prominent gurus
 C. Price itself
 D. Fundamental changes in the economy

Question 49

Markets rise when
 I. there are more buyers than sellers
 II. buyers are more aggressive than sellers
 III. sellers are afraid and demand a premium
 IV. more shares or contracts are bought than sold

A. I and II
B. II and III
C. II and IV
D. III and IV

Question 50

When the trend is down,
  I. short sellers tend to increase their positions
  II. longs tend to quit in disgust
  III. longs agree to buy only at a steep discount
  IV. short sellers are willing to sell at a lower price

  A. I
  B. I and II
  C. I, II, and III
  D. I, II, III, and IV

Question 51

A price shock during an uptrend
  I. is a sudden jump in price
  II. is a sudden drop in price
  III. makes bulls feel vulnerable
  IV. frightens the bears

  A. I and III
  B. II and III
  C. II and IV
  D. I and IV

Question 52

A price shock interrupts a rally, but prices recover. When prices rise to a new peak, several indicators reach a lower peak. This pattern is called a
  A. bullish divergence
  B. sudden drop in price

C. bearish divergence

D. sudden rise in price

Question 53

Match the descriptions with the type of trader described.

1. A trader who studies crop reports, industry utilization rates, and actions of the Federal Reserve
2. A trader who uses a computer to search for repetitive price patterns
3. A trader who listens to the advice of gurus on free financial shows
4. A trader who hears from his father-in-law about an upcoming takeover

A. A hunch player

B. A fundamental analyst

C. A technical analyst

D. An insider

Question 54

Technical analysis is

I. a science

II. an art

III. a looking glass that allows traders to see what they want

IV. a simple skill

A. I

B. I and II

C. I, II, and III

D. I, II, III, and IV

Question 55

The main goals of a trader/analyst are to
  I. identify the current trend
  II. forecast prices in the near future
  III. forecast long-term prices
  IV. stay objective and unemotional

  A. I and II
  B. I and IV
  C. II and III
  D. III and IV

III

Classical Chart Analysis

The early chartists had a revolutionary idea. They found they could make rational trading decisions based on price and volume data—without the fundamental economic information about the companies whose stocks they traded. That was especially important in the days when insider trading was more rampant than now.

The number of trading vehicles around the globe continues to grow. Once you understand the universal principles of charting, you can apply them to stocks, bonds, currencies, futures and options, or any other market.

As long as you have accurate data on high, low, and closing prices, augmented by information on opening prices, volume, and open interest, you can make intelligent judgments about the balance of power between bulls and bears. Then you can trade in the direction of the dominant market group and avoid joining the losers.

Answer the first three questions in this chapter. If you get fewer than two answers right, please review the recommended reading materials. If you answer two or three questions correctly, proceed to the rest of this chapter. You will be asked to make trading decisions using the charts. It may be fairly easy to recognize patterns in the middle of a chart, but it is much harder to see good trading signals as you move toward the right edge. This is where you'll have to make your trading decisions—amid the uncertainty, noise, and tension of the markets.

Questions	Trial 1	Trial 2	Trial 3	Trial 4	Trial 5
56					
57					
58					
59					
60					
61					
62					
63					
64					
65					
66					
67					
68					
69					
70					
71					
72					
73					
74					
75					
76					
77					
78					
79					
80					
Correct answers					

Question 56

Match the statements on the meanings of prices.
1. Amateurs' opinion
2. Professionals' opinion
3. Maximum power of bulls
4. Maximum power of bears

A. The high of the day
B. The low of the day
C. The closing price
D. The opening price

Question 57

Three analysts look at the same chart. One argues that the trend is up, the other that the trend is down, and the third that the trend is neutral. In all probability,
   I. one or two of these analysts may be practicing wishful thinking
   II. these analysts may not have agreed on the basic definitions of trends
   III. these analysts may be looking at different timeframes
   IV. if you were to lay a thousand analysts head to toe, they would not reach a conclusion

A. I
B. I and II
C. I, II, and III
D. I, II, III, and IV

Question 58

In trying to enter a liquid market on a quiet day, you are likely to encounter

A. higher slippage
B. higher commissions
C. lower slippage
D. lower commissions

Question 59

Which line in Figure 1 marks only the level of support?

    A
    B
    C
    D

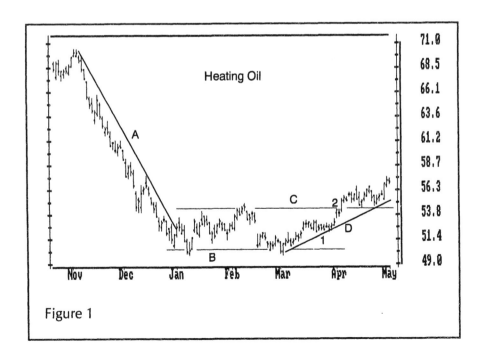

Figure 1

Question 60

Support and resistance lines should
    I. be drawn across the edges of congestion areas
    II. be drawn to touch extreme high or low prices
    III. connect highs with lows and lows with highs
    IV. connect highs with highs and lows with lows

    A. I and II
    B. II and III
    C. III and IV
    D. I and IV

Question 61

The strength of a support or resistance area depends on the
    I. number of times prices have hit that area
    II. volume of trading in that area
    III. height of that area
    IV. length of time prices have spent in that area

    A. I
    B. I and II
    C. I, II, and III
    D. I, II, III, and IV

Question 62

Prices spend several weeks in a congestion area, then close below support. To trade on the following day,
    I. sell short if prices fall to a new low, with a stop inside the congestion area
    II. go long if prices do not fall to a new low, with a stop below yesterday's low

III. sell short at the opening
IV. go long at the opening

   A. I
   B. I and II
   C. I, II, and III
   D. I, II, III, and IV

Question 63

A trader buys heating oil at point 1 in Figure 1, in the midst of a minor congestion area, with a protective stop immediately below. Heating oil rallies. At point 2, which of the following is *not* a good choice?
   A. Tighten your stop.
   B. Do nothing.
   C. Add to your position.
   D. Take partial profits.

Question 64

Identify the following by matching them with the lettered lines in Figure 2.
   1. Uptrendline
   2. Support
   3. Downtrendline
   4. Resistance

Question 65

Which of the following apply to trends and which to trading ranges?
   A. Each rally reaches a higher high.
   B. Each decline stops at approximately the same level.

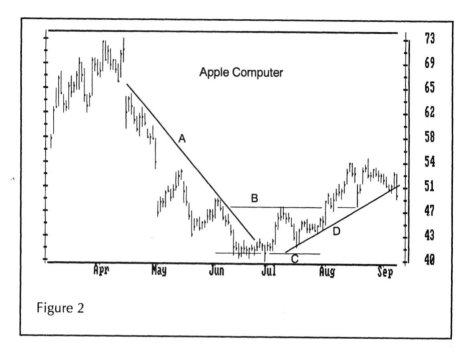

Figure 2

C. Buy weakness, sell strength.
D. Buy strength, sell short weakness.
E. Add to your positions.
F. Run at the first sign of a reversal.

Question 66

Examine the last four trading days in Figure 2 and match the statements to the days.

1. A wide-range move indicates that the uptrend may be over; stand aside.
2. A wide-range move indicates strength; hold longs, move up stops to protect some profit.
3. Prices are steady at the rising trendline; hold longs.
4. Prices decline into support at the rising trendline; the day's narrow range shows that bears are weak; go long.

A. Fourth day from the end
B. Third day from the end
C. Next to the last day
D. Last day

Question 67

Which of the following tactics work well in uptrends?
   I. Buy breakouts to new highs.
   II. Buy pullbacks into support.
   III. Buy when profits on your previous long position are protected by
   a stop.
   IV. Buy when prices take out the previous low.

   A. I
   B. I and II
   C. I, II, and III
   D. I, II, III, and IV

Question 68

Which trendline shown in Figure 3 is better, and why?
   A. Trendline 1, because it connects the bottoms of declines in an
      uptrend
   B. Trendline 2, because it connects the bottoms of congestion areas
   C. Trendline 1, because it remains inviolate long into the uptrend
   D. Trendline 2, because it has more points of contact with prices

Question 69

Which of the following does *not* apply to "tails," marked "T" in
Figure 3?
   A. When a tail points down, go short.
   B. Tails are single bars protruding from compact congestion areas.

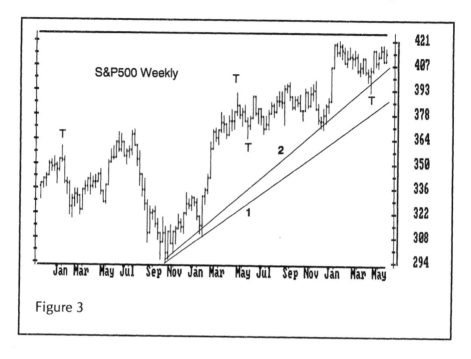

Figure 3

C. When a tail points up, it gives a sell signal.
D. Markets usually recoil from their "tails."

Question 70

Rate the importance of these features of trendlines.
    I. The number of contacts between prices and a trendline
    II. Expanding volume when prices move away from a trendline
    III. The slope of a trendline
    IV. The duration of a trendline

    A. I, II, III, IV
    B. II, III, IV, I
    C. III, IV, I, II
    D. IV, I, II, III

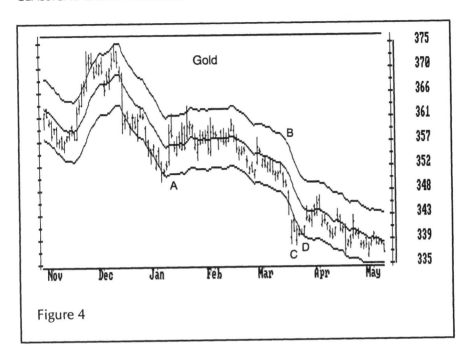

Figure 4

Question 71

Which statement concerning trendline breaks is true?
  A. When prices break an uptrendline and then pull back to it from below, sell short.
  B. When prices break an uptrendline, go short immediately.
  C. When prices close below a rising trendline, the uptrend is dead.
  D. If prices rise vertically above their uptrendline, maintain stops below that trendline.

Question 72

Identify the following gaps by matching them with the letters in Figure 4.
  1. Common gap
  2. Breakaway gap
  3. Continuation gap

4. Exhaustion gap
5. Island reversal

Question 73

Overnight gaps are caused by
  I. an imbalance of buy and sell orders at the opening
  II. overseas trading
  III. the unwillingness of floor traders to buy or sell within the previous day's range
  IV. reactions to news

  A. I
  B. I and II
  C. I, II, and III
  D. I, II, III, and IV

Question 74

Match each gap with a preferred trading tactic.
  1. Common gap
  2. Upside breakaway gap
  3. Upside continuation gap
  4. Upside exhaustion gap

  A. Buy with a stop below the gap.
  B. Stand aside or fade the gap.
  C. Go short.
  D. Wait for a pullback.

Question 75

Identify the following components of a head-and-shoulders top by matching them with the appropriate letters in Figure 5.

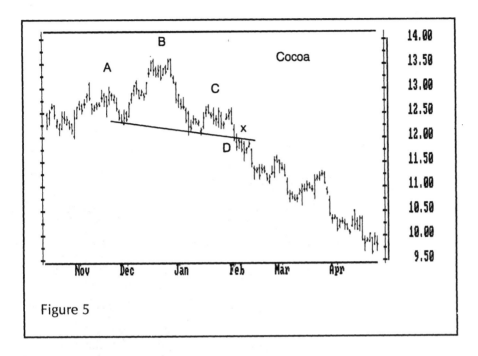

Figure 5

1. Right shoulder
2. Neckline
3. Head
4. Left shoulder

Question 76

If you sell short in area C of Figure 5,
   I. place a protective stop to cover shorts above area B
   II. place an order to go long in area B
   III. add to shorts after prices break the neckline D and pull back to it
   IV. take profits when prices slide to neckline D

   A. I
   B. I and II
   C. I, II, and III
   D. I, II, III, and IV

Question 77

Keeping in mind that markets often overshoot the downside pro-jections of head-and-shoulders tops, examine the chart of cocoa. In February, at point X in Figure 5, we can expect the market to fall at least to which level?

A. 11.00
B. 10.30
C. 9.70
D. None of the above

Question 78

Indicate which of the following statements apply to triangles (T), rectangles (R), or both?

A. A congestion area whose boundaries mark the areas of the maxi-mum power of bulls and bears
B. A congestion area whose boundaries converge
C. Early breakouts are especially significant.
D. The longer it lasts, the more significant the breakout.

Question 79

Identify the following patterns in Figure 6.

1. Symmetrical triangle
2. Ascending triangle
3. Descending triangle
4. Rectangle

Question 80

The trend is up, and prices are in the midst of triangle B in Figure 6. A trader can

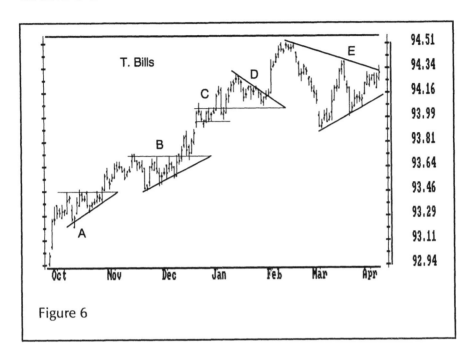

T. Bills

Figure 6

I. place an order to buy on a breakout above the upper boundary
II. place an order to buy at the lower boundary
III. wait for an upside breakout, then go long on a pullback
IV. cancel all sell orders

A. I
B. I and II
C. I, II, and III
D. I, II, III, and IV

IV

Computerized Technical Analysis

A trader has more competitors today than ever before. The markets have grown, and data is instantly disseminated around the globe. Computers can help you deal with this torrential flow of market information and get an edge over your competitors.

Computerized technical analysis requires an investment in technology. It can make your trading more objective. Indicators do not lie — when they are up, they are clearly up, and when they are down, they are clearly down.

Begin by answering the first three questions in this chapter. If you get fewer than two answers right, please review the recommended reading materials. If you answer two or three questions correctly, proceed to the rest of this chapter. If you own technical analysis software, feel free to use it while answering the questions in this chapter.

Questions	Trial 1	Trial 2	Trial 3	Trial 4	Trial 5
81					
82					
83					
84					
85					
86					
87					
88					
89					
90					
91					
92					
93					
94					
95					
96					
97					
98					
99					
100					
101					
102					
103					
104					
105					
106					
107					
108					
109					
110					
111					
112					
Correct answers					

Question 81

Computerized technical analysis
   I. is more objective than classical charting
   II. allows traders to forecast the future
   III. removes emotions from trading
   IV. assures success in trading

   A. I
   B. I and II
   C. I, II, and III
   D. I, II, III, and IV

Question 82

Becoming a computerized trader involves acquiring a computer, software, and data for analysis. What is the preferred order for selecting them?
   A. Data, software, computer
   B. Software, computer, data
   C. Computer, data, software
   D. Does not really matter

Question 83

Match the descriptions of trading software packages with their types.
   1. You feed this type of program current market data and receive specific buy and sell signals.
   2. Same as above, but you can choose a longer or shorter period for analysis, as well as the relative weights of two indicators.
   3. A collection of charting options and indicators

   A. Gray box
   B. Toolbox
   C. Black box

Question 84

Match the descriptions with the names of the three main groups of technical indicators.
1. Provides insights into mass psychology of the markets
2. Catches turning points in flat markets but give premature and dangerous signals when the markets begin to trend
3. Works best when markets are moving but gives bad signals when the markets are flat

A. Oscillators
B. Trend-following indicators
C. Miscellaneous indicators

Question 85

A stock has closed at 23, 22, 21, 20, 23, and 24 during the past 6 days. What is its 5-day simple moving average on the last day?
A. 21
B. 22
C. 23
D. None of the above

Question 86

Exponential moving averages work better than simple MAs for all of the following reasons, *except* EMAs
A. are easier to calculate by hand
B. respond to changes in prices faster
C. do not jump in response to old data
D. track the mass mood of the crowd more closely

Question 87

The most important message of an exponential moving average is
A. the width of its time window
B. its ability to rise to a new peak

C. its ability to fall to a new low
D. the direction of its slope

Question 88

Match these strategies to the appropriate lettered sections of Figure 7.
1. Trade only from the long side.
2. Trade only from the short side.
3. Go long slightly below the exponential moving average.
4. Go short slightly above the exponential moving average.

Question 89

Match the following tactics to the numbered areas of Figure 7.
A. Go long, with a protective stop slightly below the latest low.
B. Go short, with a protective stop slightly above the latest high.
C. Liquidate positions and stand aside—the market may be turning.

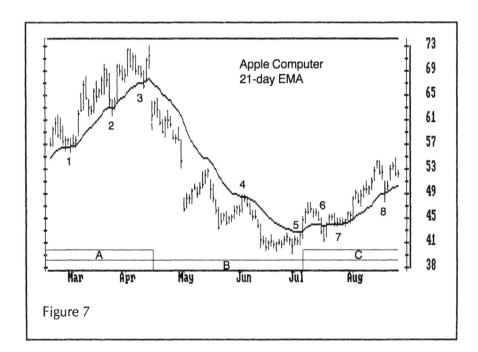

Figure 7

Question 90

Which of the following statements regarding MACD (Moving Average Convergence-Divergence) are true?
  I. The fast line of MACD reflects short-term bullishness or bearishness.
  II. The slow line of MACD reflects long-term bullishness or bearishness.
  III. When the fast line is above the slow line, bulls are in control.
  IV. When the fast line is below the slow line, bears are in control.

  A. I and II
  B. III and IV
  C. None of the above
  D. I, II, III, and IV

Question 91

Which statement about MACD-Histogram is *not* true?
  A. It measures the spread between the fast and slow MACD lines.
  B. When it rises, it shows that bulls are in control.
  C. It forecasts higher or lower prices ahead.
  D. It identifies the dominant market group.

Question 92

To which lettered areas in Figure 8 do these statements apply?
  1. MACD-Histogram rises to a new high—expect prices to retest or exceed the latest price peak.
  2. MACD-Histogram falls to a new low—expect prices to retest or exceed the latest bottom.
  3. A bearish divergence
  4. A bullish divergence

Question 93

At the right edge of Figure 8, MACD-Histogram is telling us
  A. that the latest price peak is likely to be retested or exceeded; go long immediately
  B. that bears are in control; go short immediately

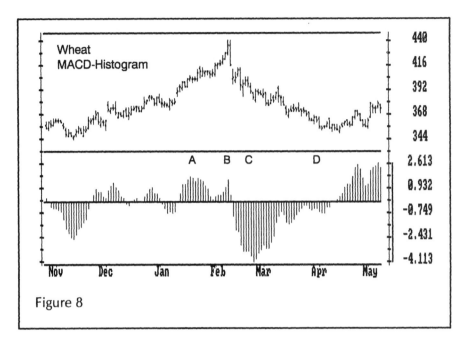

Figure 8

C. to buy the next pullback
D. to sell short the next rally

Question 94

Which of the following statements describe Directional Movement?
   A. the part of today's bar that is above the previous day's bar
   B. the part of today's bar that is below the previous day's bar
   C. the largest part of today's bar outside of the previous day's bar
   D. none of the above

Question 95

Match these actions with the areas in Figure 9 marked by letters.
   1. When the Directional Indicator turns down from above both Directional Lines, take at least partial profits.
   2. When the Directional Indicator penetrates above the lower Directional Line, trade in the direction of the upper Directional Line.

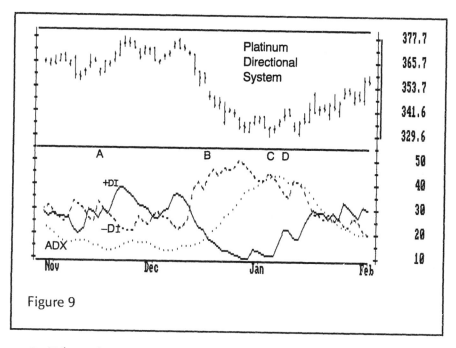

Figure 9

3. When the Directional Indicator rises above both Directional Lines, the trend is mature and ready for a reversal.
4. Do not use a trend-following method when the Directional Indicator is below both Directional Lines.

Question 96

At the right edge of Figure 9, the Directional System is telling us to
   I. go long
   II. go short
   III. stand aside
   IV. use other indicators

   A. I and III
   B. II and III
   C. II and IV
   D. III and IV

Question 97

Oscillators can help traders accomplish all of the following *except*
  A. catch all tops and bottoms
  B. identify the extremes of mass pessimism and optimism
  C. measure the speed of market moves
  D. bet against deviations and for a return to normalcy

Question 98

Match the statements about oscillators.
  1. High level of an oscillator—associated with tops
  2. Low level of an oscillator—associated with bottoms
  3. A line across the peaks of an oscillator
  4. A line across the lows of an oscillator

  A. Lower reference line
  B. Oversold
  C. Overbought
  D. Upper reference line

Question 99

When an oscillator reaches its highest peak in several months, which of the following is *least* likely?
  A. The rally is likely to pause.
  B. Prices are likely to rise to a higher high.
  C. Shorting signals are best ignored.
  D. Prices are likely to drop.

Question 100

With the market in a downtrend, an oscillator, such as 7-day Momentum in Figure 10, identifies
  I. shorting opportunities
  II. selling areas
  III. buying opportunities
  IV. short-covering areas

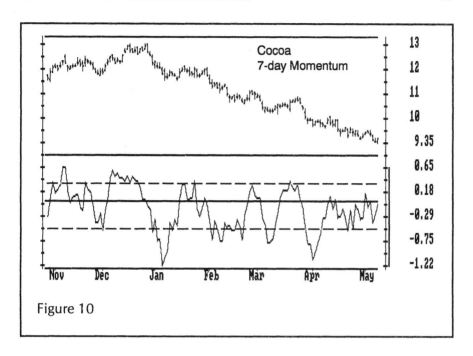

Figure 10

A. I and II
B. III and IV
C. I, II, III, and IV
D. None of the above

Question 101

Divergences between indicators and prices give some of the most powerful buy and sell signals in technical analysis. Identify the following by matching them with the lettered pairs of graphs in Figure 11.

1. Class A bullish divergence
2. Class A bearish divergence
3. Class B bullish divergence
4. Class B bearish divergence
5. Class C bullish divergence
6. Class C bearish divergence

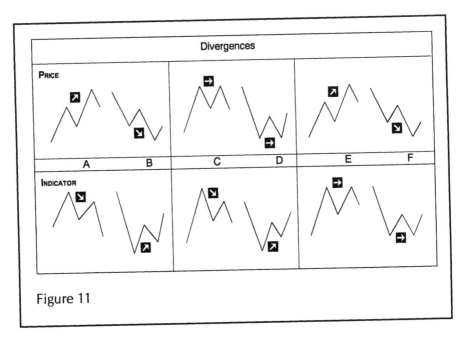

Figure 11

Question 102

Williams %R measures the placement of each closing price relative to the

    A. recent high

    B. recent low

    C. recent range

    D. moving average

Question 103

Identify the following formations of Williams %R by matching them with the letters in Figure 12.

    1. Overbought

    2. Oversold

    3. Bullish divergence

    4. Bearish divergence

    5. Failure swing

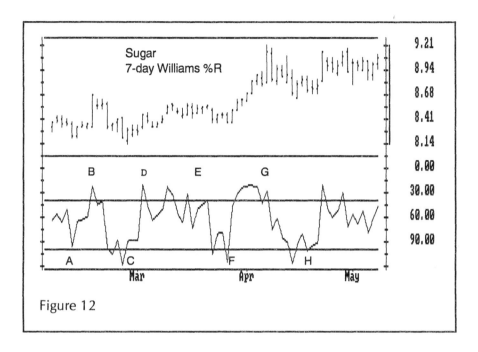

Figure 12

Question 104

The right edge of Figure 12 tells us that
   I. Wm %R is rising; go long
   II. Wm %R is tracing a Class B bearish divergence; go short
   III. the uptrend that began in March is intact; go long
   IV. the uptrend stalled a month ago; go short

   A. I and III
   B. II and IV
   C. I, II, III, and IV
   D. None of the above

Question 105

To set the width of the Stochastic time window,
   I. make it 5 days
   II. make it half the market cycle

III. make it 21 days

IV. when in doubt, make it shorter

A. I and II

B. II and III

C. II and IV

D. I and IV

Question 106

Match the statements about Stochastic.

1. Maximum power of bulls for the past 5 days
2. Capacity of bulls or bears to close the market in their favor
3. Maximum power of bears for the past 5 days
4. Consensus of value at the end of the trading day

A. Last closing price

B. 5-day Stochastic

C. 5-day high

D. 5-day low

Question 107

Identify the following formations of Stochastic by matching them with the appropriate letters in Figure 13.

1. Overbought
2. Oversold
3. Bullish divergence
4. Bearish divergence
5. Failure swing

Question 108

At the right edge of Figure 13, the trading message is,

A. Stochastic is overbought; go short

B. Stochastic is rising; go long

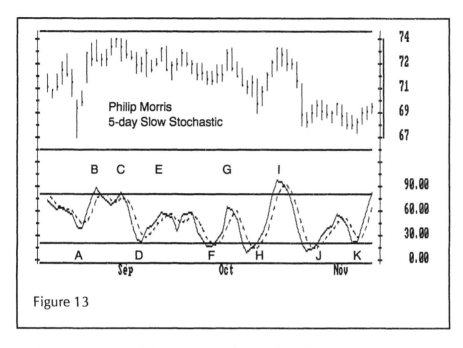

Figure 13

C. the downtrend that began in August is still in force; go short
D. stand aside

Question 109

Each price represents a momentary consensus of value among all market participants. The closing price represents the most important consensus of the day because

I. markets tend to be dominated by professional traders at closing time
II. the settlement of traders' accounts depends on closing prices
III. all traders who have open positions are stuck with them until the market reopens
IV. closing prices are published in many newspapers

A. I
B. I and II
C. I, II, and III
D. I, II, III, and IV

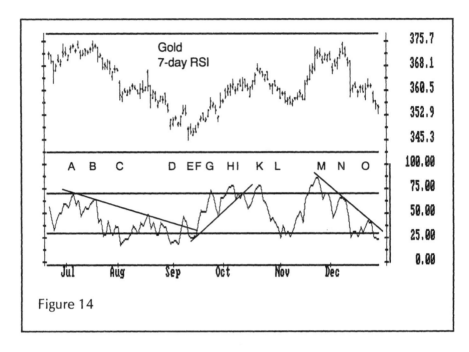

Figure 14

Question 110

Identify these formations of RSI (Relative Strength Index) in Figure 14.
1. Overbought
2. Oversold
3. Bullish divergence
4. Bearish divergence
5. Trendline break

Question 111

What sets the Relative Strength Index (RSI) apart from most other indicators?
I. It is based exclusively on closing prices.
II. It shows more divergences than other indicators.

III. It identifies overbought and oversold conditions in the markets.
IV. It lends itself especially well to trendline analysis.

   A. I and II
   B. II and III
   C. III and IV
   D. I and IV

Question 112

At the right edge of Figure 14, RSI is telling us that
   A. gold is oversold; hold shorts or take profits on short positions
   B. the trends of gold and RSI are down; go short
   C. there is a bullish divergence; go long
   D. signals are mixed; stand aside for now

V

The Neglected Essentials

Beginning analysts and traders pay attention only to prices. They watch their trading vehicles go up or down, and become mesmerized by their motion. They may even count dollars at every uptick and downtick.

Experienced analysts can see much deeper into the markets by comparing changes in prices to the volume of transactions. They also relate every price change to the length of time it took to effect it. Open interest provides an additional insight into the balance of power between bulls and bears.

Answer the first three questions in this chapter. If you get fewer than two answers right, please review the recommended reading materials. If you answer two or three questions correctly, proceed to the rest of this chapter. If you do not trade futures or options and do not wish to study open interest, skip the questions about open interest and add 5 points to your score.

Questions	Trial 1	Trial 2	Trial 3	Trial 4	Trial 5
113					
114					
115					
116					
117					
118					
119					
120					
121					
122					
123					
124					
125					
126					
127					
128					
129					
130					
131					
132					
133					
Correct answers					

Question 113

Which of these statements apply to volume?
   I. Number of trades during a selected time period
   II. Number of shares or contracts traded
   III. Number of price changes during a time period
   IV. Activity of traders and investors

   A. I
   B. II and III
   C. IV
   D. I, II, III, and IV

Question 114

Volume reflects all of the following *except*
   A. How market participants will react to future price changes
   B. How many winners and losers are active in the market
   C. Whether masses of losers are standing pat or running
   D. The degree of emotional involvement among traders

Question 115

The market has been rising for several months in an orderly pattern of rallies and shallow declines; a new rally is in progress. Match the statements about volume.
   1. Volume is slightly higher than during the previous rally.
   2. Volume is double what it was during the previous rally.
   3. Volume is half of what it was during the previous rally.
   4. Volume is approximately the same as during the previous rally.

   A. Bears are panicking; take at least partial profits on long positions.
   B. The uptrend is healthy; hold longs or add to them.

C. The uptrend is running out of steam; take at least partial profits on long positions.

D. The uptrend is healthy; hold longs.

Question 116

Identify the following patterns of volume by matching them with the appropriate letters in Figure 15.

1. Volume shrinks while prices reach a new high; expect a top; sell longs or tighten stops.

2. Volume soars as prices decline; expect a climax bottom; take profits on short positions and get ready to go long.

3. Prices rally on expanding volume; expect higher prices ahead; go long or add to longs.

4. Volume expands while prices decline; expect lower prices ahead; maintain short positions or add to them.

5. Volume shrinks while prices fall to a new low; expect a bottom; take profits on short positions or tighten stops.

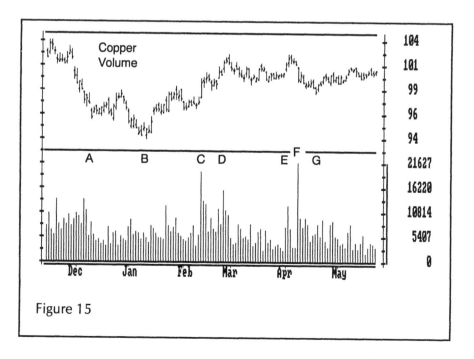

Figure 15

Question 117

At the right edge of Figure 15, the pattern of volume and prices shows that
   A. prices are rising from their April climax bottom; go long
   B. prices are near the top of a two week range, while volume is lower; go short
   C. volume has been rising during the latest rally; go long
   D. stand aside for now

Question 118

On-Balance Volume (OBV)
   I. confirms bear moves when it falls to a new low
   II. tracks the running total of traders' emotional commitments
   III. often reaches a new peak before a new peak in price
   IV. rises whenever the market closes lower

   A. I
   B. I and II
   C. I, II, and III
   D. I, II, III, and IV

Question 119

Identify the following formations of prices and On-Balance Volume (OBV) by matching them with the appropriate letters in Figure 16.
   1. A bearish divergence; sell longs and go short
   2. A new low of OBV; expect lower prices ahead; trade from the short side
   3. A new peak of OBV; expect higher prices ahead; trade from the long side

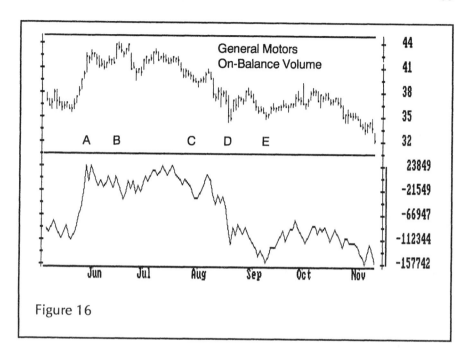

Figure 16

Question 120

At the right edge of Figure 16, OBV tells us that
- A. the downtrend of OBV that began in September is intact; go short
- B. OBV is not confirming the new low in prices; go long
- C. OBV is in a trading range—stand aside
- D. none of the above

Question 121

Match the statements about Accumulation/Distribution.
- 1. Prices open below the previous day's close and close lower.
- 2. Prices open above the previous day's open and close higher.
- 3. Prices open above the previous day's close, but close at the lows.
- 4. Prices open below the previous day's close, but close at the highs.

A. Amateurs relatively bearish, professionals relatively bullish
B. Amateurs relatively bullish, professionals relatively bearish
C. Amateurs and professionals bullish
D. Amateurs and professionals bearish

Question 122

The Chicago Board of Trade reports that open interest in soybeans stands at 120,000 contracts. This means that
A. 60,000 contracts are held by the longs and 60,000 owed by the shorts
B. 120,000 contracts are held by the longs and 120,000 owed by the shorts
C. 240,000 contracts are held by the longs and 240,000 owed by the shorts
D. There is not enough information to decide how many contracts are held by the longs or owed by the shorts

Question 123

Match the events with their effects on open interest.
1. A trader who is long sells to another who is short.
2. A new bear enters the market and sells to an earlier bear who buys to cover his shorts.
3. A new bull enters the market and buys from an earlier bull who sells his position.
4. A new buyer and a new seller trade with each other.

A. Open interest increases.
B. Open interest decreases.
C. Open interest stays unchanged.
D. Not enough information to decide.

Question 124

Rising open interest shows that
    I. bulls are confident and aggressive
    II. the supply of losers is growing
    III. the trend is likely to continue
    IV. bears are confident and aggressive

    A. I
    B. I and II
    C. I, II, and III
    D. I, II, III, and IV

Question 125

Identify the following patterns by matching them with the appropriate letters in Figure 17.
    1. Rising open interest confirms the uptrend; go long.
    2. Flat open interest shows that bulls have stopped exiting; cover shorts.
    3. Falling open interest and prices show that bulls are being washed out of the market but bears are skittish; go short with tight stops.
    4. A bearish divergence; go short

Question 126

At the right edge of Figure 17, open interest tells us that
    I. prices and open interest are down; bulls are running; go short
    II. prices and open interest are down; bears show little confidence in the downtrend; go long
    III. the trend is moving down in an orderly fashion; get ready to short into the next minor rally
    IV. prices and open interest are approaching the levels from which a rally sprang in December; place an order to buy above the latest peak

A. I
B. II
C. III
D. III and IV

Question 127

The Herrick Payoff Index (HPI) detects accumulation and distribution by measuring changes in
  I. prices
 II. volume
III. open interest
IV. a moving average

A. I
B. I and II

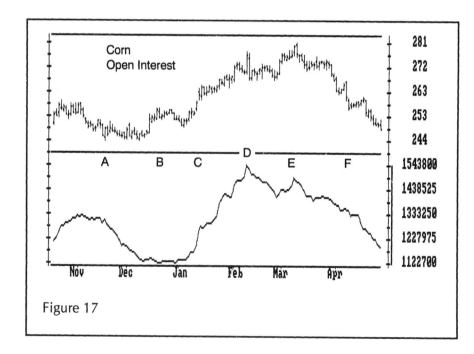

Figure 17

C. I, II, and III
D. I, II, III, and IV

Question 128

Identify the following signals by matching them with the appropriate letters on the chart of the Herrick Payoff Index shown in Figure 18.
1. New low; downtrend is intact; go short
2. Bearish divergence; get ready to trade short
3. New peak; uptrend is intact; go long
4. Bullish divergence; get ready to trade long

Question 129

The right edge of Figure 18 tells us that
  I. HPI is at a new high; go long
  II. prices are at the top of their trading range; go short
  III. HPI is above its centerline; go long
  IV. HPI is overbought; go short

A. I and III
B. II and IV
C. I, II, III, and IV
D. None of the above

Question 130

The presence of cycles in market data depends on
  I. changes in the economic fundamentals
  II. greed in good times and fear in bad times among producers and consumers
  III. swings between pessimism and optimism among traders
  IV. planetary influences

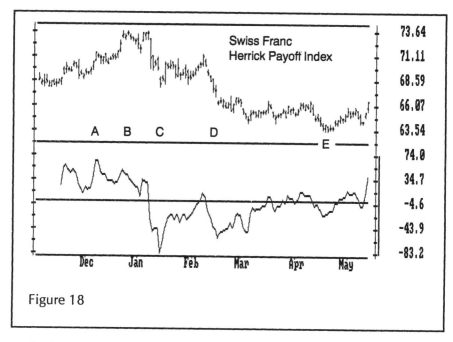

Figure 18

A. I
B. I and II
C. I, II, and III
D. I, II, III, and IV

Question 131

Bonds advance for 7 days, decline for 3 days, advance for 8 days, decline for 4 days, advance again for 6 days, and start declining. When should you start looking for a buying opportunity?

A. In about 3 days
B. In about 5 days
C. It is too late to buy, the advance has gone on for too long.
D. The trend is up; buy immediately.

Question 132

Identify the "indicator seasons" by matching them with the appropriate letters in Figure 19.

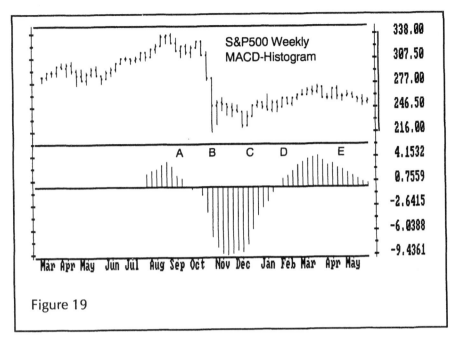

Figure 19

1. Spring; go long
2. Summer; start taking profits on longs
3. Autumn; go short
4. Winter; start taking profits on shorts

Question 133

Traders can analyze markets in greater depth by looking at them in two timeframes. Which of the following combinations makes the most sense?

    A. Weekly and daily
    B. Monthly and daily
    C. Yearly and daily
    D. Yearly and weekly

VI

Stock Market Indicators

Stock market analysts have several indicators not available to traders in other markets. You can analyze the stock market as a whole using special tools that show whether the market is bullish or bearish. You can translate that knowledge into trading decisions in individual stocks, index futures, or options.

Many old stock market indicators have become distorted as the stock markets have changed in the last two decades. Only a handful of stock market indicators, notably New High–New Low index (NH-NL) and Traders' Index (TRIN), continue to perform as well today as they have in the past. Learning to use them can help improve your trading.

Answer one or two questions from the beginning of this chapter, dealing with NH-NL, and one or two from the middle, dealing with TRIN. If you get fewer than half the answers right, please review the recommended reading materials. Otherwise, proceed to the rest of this chapter. Afterward, apply what you learned to your current stock market position.

Questions	Trial 1	Trial 2	Trial 3	Trial 4	Trial 5
134					
135					
136					
137					
138					
139					
140					
141					
142					
Correct answers					

Question 134

New High–New Low Index (NH-NL)
  I. measures the number of new highs on any given day
  II. tracks the number of the weakest stocks on the exchange
  III. measures the number of new lows on any given day
  IV. tracks the number of the strongest stocks on the exchange

  A. I and III
  B. II and IV
  C. I, II, III, and IV
  D. None of the above

Question 135

Match the statements about the New High–New Low Index (NH-NL) with what they indicate about the market.
  1. NH-NL is positive, rises to a new high for the move.
  2. Stock market falls to a new low, NH-NL traces a higher bottom.
  3. NH-NL is negative, declines to a new low for the move.
  4. Stock market reaches a new peak, NH-NL traces a lower peak.

  A. Bearish leadership is strong; trade from the short side.
  B. Bearish divergence shows that bulls are becoming weak; start taking profits on long positions and look to go short.
  C. Bullish divergence shows that bears are becoming weak; start taking profits on short positions and look to go long.
  D. Bullish leadership is strong; trade from the long side.

Question 136

Identify the following patterns by matching them with the appropriate letters on the chart of the New High–New Low Index (NH-NL) shown in Figure 20.

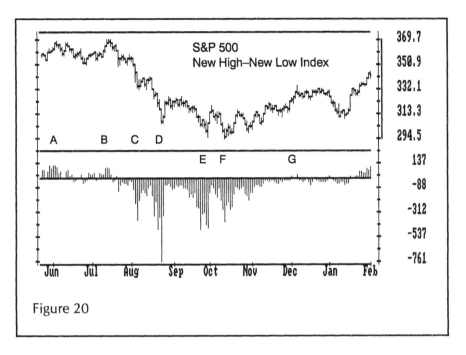

Figure 20

1. A bullish divergence; get ready to go long
2. A bearish divergence; get ready to go short
3. Bulls predominate; trade from the long side
4. Bears predominate; trade from the short side

Question 137

At the right edge of Figure 20, NH-NL tells us that
   I. NH-NL is overbought; sell short
   II. NH-NL is positive and rising; go long
   III. no bullish divergence is present; stand aside
   IV. trading signals are mixed; stand aside

   A. I
   B. II
   C. III and IV
   D. None of the above

Question 138

When the volume of advancing stocks rises out of proportion to their number for several days in a row, it shows that
  A. the crowd is very bullish; go long
  B. the market is overbought; go short
  C. this bullishness is not sustainable—expect a top
  D. this market behavior is abnormal—stand aside

Question 139

Which of the following does *not* apply to the Traders' Index (TRIN)?
  A. TRIN works better when smoothed with an exponential moving average.
  B. TRIN is normally less than 1 because people tend to be more bullish than bearish.
  C. TRIN shows clear-cut overbought and oversold levels.
  D. TRIN identifies the extremes of mass optimism and pessimism.

Question 140

Identify the following patterns by matching them with the appropriate letters on the chart of the Traders' Index shown in Figure 21.
  1. TRIN is overbought; go short when it leaves its overbought zone.
  2. TRIN is oversold; go long when it leaves its oversold zone.
  3. A bearish divergence; go short
  4. A bullish divergence; go long

Question 141

The right edge of Figure 21 tells us that
  A. no trading opportunity is present at the moment
  B. TRIN is falling, bears are in control; go short
  C. TRIN is near the level associated with bottoms; go long

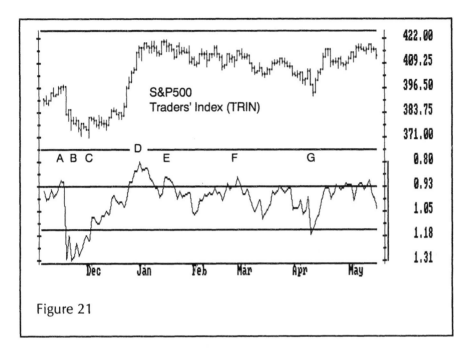

Figure 21

Question 142

The Advance/Decline line
   I. tracks the numbers of rising and falling stocks
   II. indicates strength when it rises to a new high and weakness
   when it falls to a new low
   III. the pattern of its peaks and valleys is more important than its
   level
   IV. indicates when volume confirms price moves

   A. I
   B. I and II
   C. I, II, and III
   D. I, II, III, and IV

VII

Psychological Indicators

Huge crowds of traders place their buy and sell orders in the financial markets. The actions of bulls and bears create powerful waves of mass optimism and pessimism, fear and greed, disappointment and joy. These emotional tides attract bystanders and bring even more buying and selling into the markets. The fundamental economic factors may rule the markets in the long run, but mass market psychology determines their intermediate- and short-term course.

Several indicators take the pulse of the market crowd. They provide some startling insights and help identify important trading opportunities. They are especially important to those who trade in the United States, where several advisory services track these indicators. An overseas trader could profit from trying to develop similar tools in his own country.

Answer three questions taken at random from this chapter. If you get fewer than two answers right, please review the recommended reading materials. If you answer two or three questions correctly, proceed to the rest of this chapter.

Questions	Trial 1	Trial 2	Trial 3	Trial 4	Trial 5
143					
144					
145					
146					
147					
148					
149					
Correct answers					

Question 143

When an overwhelming majority of market participants turn bullish,
   I. the market is near a top; sell and look to go short
   II. the uptrend is strong; go long
   III. there are not enough new buyers to support the market
   IV. bulls are strong and confident

   A. I
   B. I and III
   C. II
   D. II and IV

Question 144

A futures or options market enters a powerful uptrend, and bullish consensus rises to 75 percent. This means that
   A. an average bear has three times as much money as an average bull
   B. an average bear has approximately as much money as an average bull
   C. an average bull has three times as much money as an average bear
   D. there is not enough information to decide whether an average bull or bear has more money

Question 145

A rich harvest sends corn into a bear market. As futures grind their way down, bullish consensus falls to 20 percent. This means that
   A. an average bull has five times as much money as an average bear

B. an average bull has approximately as much money as an average bear

C. an average bear has four times as much money as an average bull

D. an average bull has four times as much money as an average bear

Question 146

Your newspaper reports that coffee prices are at their highest level in six years; TV news shows snow in coffee-growing Brazil; and your mother-in-law tells you she bought 5 lbs of instant coffee before its price rises any higher. Your response as a trader is to plan to

A. go long coffee futures or long calls

B. go short coffee futures or long puts

C. go long cocoa futures, as a play on a catch-up move with coffee

D. buy gold because the rise in coffee is a sign of inflation

Question 147

Match the statements about traders' positions.

I. Position limits

II. Reporting requirements

III. Inside information

IV. Hedging

A. The level at which your trade gets reported to a government agency

B. Taking a futures position to offset a position in an actual commodity

C. Can be exceeded by commercials

D. Legal in the futures markets

Question 148

Match the statements about different groups of market participants.

 I. Small speculators
 II. Large speculators
 III. Commercials
 IV. Company insiders

 A. Hold contracts in excess of reporting levels
 B. Hedge business risks
 C. Officers or large stockholders
 D. The group of "Wrong-way Corrigans"

Question 149

A bear market is 11 months old; the company whose stock you follow reports lower quarterly earnings; its two vice presidents and a major shareholder buy its stock; the stock is $1 above its low for the year. As an investor, you

 A. go short immediately (the bear market is in force)
 B. go long immediately (insider buying)
 C. stay away from the market until the next bull market starts
 D. start buying, accumulating a long position

VIII

New Indicators

To succeed in trading you need to use better tools than other traders. You also need to be more disciplined than the rest of the trading crowd. You have to reach for every possible advantage in the markets.

This chapter tests your knowledge of two new tools—Force Index and Elder-ray. They can help you find good entry points into trades, decide when to add to winning positions, and see when it's time to take profits.

Any indicator or trading system can work for you only when you make it your own, adjust it to fit your unique trading style. Once you learn to use the Force Index and Elder-ray, think about creating your own tools.

Answer one or two questions from the beginning of this chapter, dealing with Elder-ray, and one or two from the middle, dealing with the Force Index. If you get fewer than half the answers right, please review the recommended reading materials. Otherwise, proceed to the rest of this chapter.

Questions	Trial 1	Trial 2	Trial 3	Trial 4	Trial 5
150					
151					
152					
153					
154					
155					
156					
157					
158					
159					
160					
Correct answers					

Question 150

Match the statements about Elder-ray.

    I. Maximum power of bears
    II. Average consensus of value
    III. Maximum power of bulls
    IV. Day's most important consensus of value

    A. High of the day
    B. Low of the day
    C. Closing price
    D. Moving average

Question 151

Match the statements about Bull Power and Bear Power.

    I. The exponential moving average minus the high of the day
    II. The low of the day minus the exponential moving average
    III. The exponential moving average minus the low of the day
    IV. The high of the day minus the exponential moving average

    A. Bull Power
    B. Bear Power
    C. Both Bull Power and Bear Power
    D. Neither

Question 152

Elder-ray

    I. identifies the relative power of bulls and bears
    II. identifies the trend of the market
    III. flags buying and selling points
    IV. can serve as an automatic trading system

A. I
B. I and II
C. I, II, and III
D. I, II, III, and IV

Question 153

Match the patterns of Elder-ray with the trading signals they give.
1. Bear Power shows a bullish divergence.
2. EMA is down; Bull Power is positive but falling.
3. Bull Power shows a bearish divergence.
4. EMA is up, Bear Power is negative but rising.

A. Go long.
B. Go short.
C. Sell longs.
D. Cover shorts.

Question 154

Identify the following patterns by matching them with the appropriate letters on the chart of Elder-ray shown in Figure 22.
1. EMA is flat; Bear Power traces a massive bullish divergence; wait for an upturn to buy.
2. EMA is down; Bear Power traces a bullish divergence; cover shorts.
3. EMA is up; Bear Power is negative; go long.
4. EMA is down; Bull Power is positive; go short.

Question 155

At the right edge of Figure 22, we are long and Elder-ray is telling us

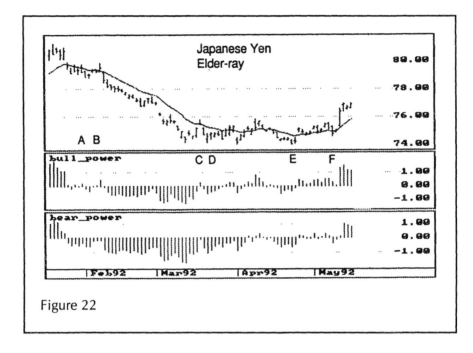

Figure 22

A. to hold longs purchased in area F and move up stops to protect
   profits
B. that Bull Power is weakening; take profits on long positions
C. that both Bull and Bear Power are overextended to the upside; go
   short
D. to stand aside; no clear trade is indicated

Question 156

When prices change, which factors indicate the force of their
move?
   I. Distance
   II. Volume
   III. Direction
   IV. Related markets

A. I
B. I and II
C. I, II, and III
D. I, II, III, and IV

Question 157

The formula for Force Index is
A. $Close_{today} \cdot (Volume_{today} - Volume_{yesterday})$
B. $Close_{today} \cdot (Volume_{today} + Volume_{yesterday})$
C. $Volume_{today} \cdot (Close_{today} + Close_{yesterday})$
D. $Volume_{today} \cdot (Close_{today} - Close_{yesterday})$

Question 158

Why smooth Force Index with a moving average?
I. The histogram of daily Force Index is too jagged.
II. A 2-day EMA of Force Index helps find entry points into the markets.
III. A 13-day EMA of Force Index helps find major shifts in the force of bulls and bears.
IV. Divergences between smoothed Force Index and prices identify turning points in the markets.

A. I
B. I and II
C. I, II, and III
D. I, II, III, and IV

Question 159

Identify the following patterns by matching them with the appropriate letters on the chart of Force Index smoothed with a 13-day exponential moving average shown in Figure 23.

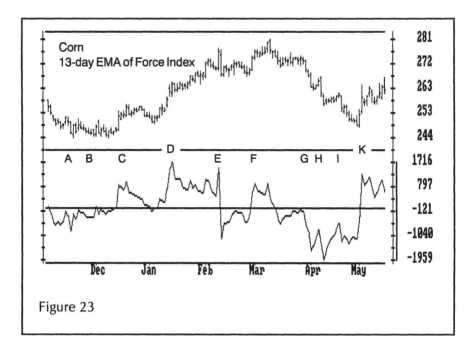

Figure 23

1. A new high for the upmove; hold longs or add to long positions on the next reaction
2. A bearish divergence; sell longs and go short
3. A new low for the downmove; hold shorts or add to short positions on the next rally
4. A bullish divergence; cover shorts and go long

Question 160

At the right edge of Figure 23, the 13-day EMA of Force Index tells us that

    I. Force Index has reached a new peak; expect higher prices ahead; go long

    II. Force Index is tracing a bearish divergence; go short

    III. the trend is up; Force Index is positive; buy dips

    IV. the market is too high; Force Index is declining; sell

A. I
B. I and III
C. II
D. II and IV

IX

Trading Systems

What is a trading system? Is it a magic device that can be fine-tuned using old data and then "put on automatic," effortlessly pulling profits out of the markets? Or is it simply a decision tree, a mechanism that flags dangers and focuses your attention on the most profitable opportunities?

A trading system is developed in the quiet of your office, away from the noise of the markets. When you trade, your system quietly reminds you what to do in the marketplace. A well-designed system protects you from your own impulsiveness, especially when the tide of mass emotion may be sweeping you off your feet.

This chapter tests your knowledge of several trading systems that have stood the test of time. While you are answering these questions, think about whether to start trading with one or more of these systems or simply to use them as a springboard for developing your own system.

Answer two questions from the beginning of this chapter, dealing with the Triple Screen trading system, and two from the middle, dealing with the Parabolic or Channel trading system. If you answer two or fewer questions right, please stop and review the recommended reading materials. If you answer three or four questions right, proceed with the rest of this chapter. Go slow — it takes a lot of thinking, work, and time to develop a sensible trading system.

Questions	Trial 1	Trial 2	Trial 3	Trial 4	Trial 5
161					
162					
163					
164					
165					
166					
167					
168					
169					
170					
171					
172					
173					
174					
175					
176					
177					
178					
179					
180					
Correct answers					

Question 161

Which of the following statements can be true simultaneously in a given market?

    I. The trend is up.

    II. The trend is down.

    III. An indicator gives a buy signal.

    IV. An indicator gives a sell signal.

    A. I and III

    B. II and IV

    C. I, II, III, and IV

    D. None of the above

Question 162

When trying to find a trade on a daily chart,

    A. focus all your attention on that chart

    B. identify the trend of the weekly chart and use the daily chart to look only for trades in the direction of the weekly trend

    C. find a trade on the daily chart and check whether the weekly chart points in the same direction

    D. identify the trend of the monthly chart and use the daily chart to look only for trades in that direction

Question 163

If you use the slope of weekly MACD-Histogram as the first screen of the Triple Screen trading system and that slope is down, you may

    A. go long

    B. go short

    C. go long or stand aside

    D. go short or stand aside

Question 164

The first screen of the Triple Screen trading system points up. You are using a 5-day Stochastic as your second screen and see it rise to 85. Now you may
- A. go long immediately
- B. go short immediately
- C. wait for Stochastic to decline below 40 and then go long
- D. wait for Stochastic to decline below 40 and then go short

Question 165

The weekly trend is up, but the decline of the past few days has pushed the 2-day EMA of Force Index below zero. Your next step is to
- A. wait until both screens get in gear
- B. place an order to buy above the previous day's high
- C. place an order to sell short below the previous day's low
- D. close out any open positions

Question 166

Match the following actions, based on the 2-day EMA of Force Index, with the appropriate lettered areas on Figure 24.
- 1. Use declines below zero for buying.
- 2. Use rallies above zero for selling short.
- 3. May use declines below zero for taking profits on short positions.
- 4. May use rallies above zero for taking profits on long positions.

Question 167

At the right edge of Figure 24, the Triple Screen trading system tells us that
- I. the weekly trend is up; the daily trend is up; go long immediately
- II. the daily Force Index shows a bearish divergence; go short immediately

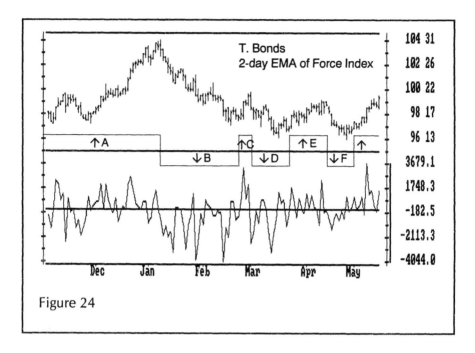

Figure 24

III. the weekly trend is up and the daily Force Index is overbought;
   wait to buy until it dips below zero

IV. prices are at the upper edge of their trading range and the daily Force
   Index shows a bearish divergence; take profits on long positions

A. I and III

B. II

C. III and IV

D. IV

Question 168

Match the statements about the Triple Screen trading system with
the action indicated.

1. The weekly trend is up; the daily trend is up.
2. The weekly trend is up; the daily trend is down.
3. The weekly trend is down; the daily trend is up.
4. The weekly trend is down; the daily trend is down.

A. Go long.
B. Go short.
C. Do not enter a new trade.

Question 169

The Parabolic trading system adjusts its stops faster or slower, depending on
   I. price action
   II. the passage of time
   III. the Acceleration Factor
   IV. the profitability of a trade

A. I
B. I and II
C. I, II, and III
D. I, II, III, and IV

Question 170

The Parabolic system
   I. forces traders to react to the passage of time
   II. helps to trade during runaway trends
   III. allows traders to reverse trading positions
   IV. protects traders from their indecision

A. I
B. I and II
C. I, II, and III

Question 171

You go long wheat during its upsurge in January and use Parabolic. It keeps you long, then reverses and takes you short in February, with a single whipsaw in March. Now, at the right edge of Figure 25, what do you choose?

A. Wheat is at a support level; go long and start calculating Parabolic from a new starting point.
B. Wheat is in a congestion area; do not use Parabolic.
C. Go short, as currently indicated by Parabolic, with a stop above the market.

Question 172

In order to construct a price channel,
    I. draw a channel line parallel to a trendline
    II. plot two lines parallel to a moving average
    III. plot one moving average of the highs and another of the lows
    IV. plot two lines whose distance from the moving average depends on volatility
    A. I
    B. I and II
    C. I, II, and III
    D. I, II, III, and IV

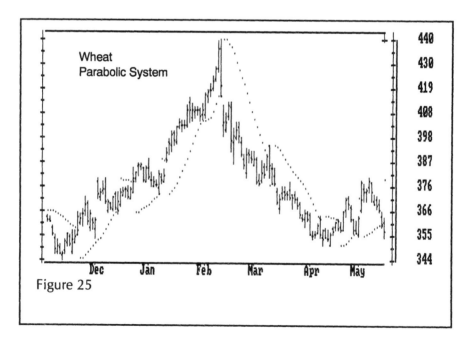

Figure 25

Question 173

The proper width of a channel
   A. is a closely guarded secret of professional traders
   B. requires a computer to calculate
   C. contains about 90 percent of prices
   D. contains about 50 percent of prices

Question 174

Match the statements about moving average channels.
   I. The market is undervalued.
   II. The market is overvalued.
   III. Depends on volatility.
   IV. The market is fairly valued.

   A. The upper channel line
   B. The moving average
   C. The lower channel line
   D. Channel coefficient

Question 175

The best way to use channels in trading is to
   A. buy upside breakouts and short downside breakouts
   B. short upside breakouts and buy downside breakouts
   C. do either of the above, depending on indicator patterns

Question 176

Which statement about channels is incorrect?
   A. Going long or short in the middle of a channel always offers attrac-
      tive trades because you buy or sell at the consensus of value.
   B. When a channel rises sharply, an upside penetration of the upper
      channel line indicates that the market is strong and should be
      bought when it returns to its moving average.

C. When a channel is relatively flat, the market is almost always a good buy near the bottom of its trading channel and a good sell near the top.

D. A breakout below the lower line of a sharply falling channel indicates that the market is weak and a pullback to the moving average will offer a shorting opportunity.

Question 177

Identify the following patterns by matching them with the appropriate letters in the chart of the CRB Index and MACD-Histogram shown in Figure 26.

1. The trend is in progress; no divergence is present.
2. A bullish divergence at the lower channel wall; go long, with a stop below the latest low.
3. A bearish divergence at the upper channel wall; go short, with a stop below the latest low.

Question 178

At the right edge of Figure 26, channels and MACD-Histogram are telling us

A. to place an order to buy at the moving average
B. that the trend is up, confirmed by MACD-Histogram; go long immediately
C. that prices have rallied above their upper channel line; go short immediately
D. to stand aside for now

Question 179

Bollinger Bands are drawn

A. parallel to a moving average
B. parallel to a trendline

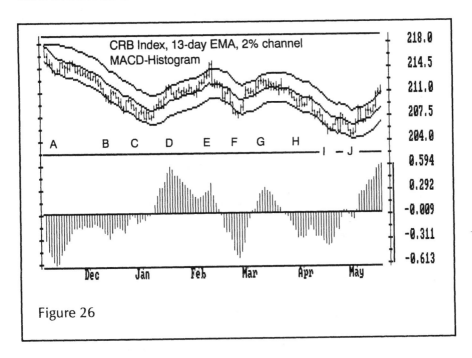

Figure 26

C. 1 standard deviation away from a moving average
D. 1 standard deviation away from a trendline

Question 180

Match the following statements about Bollinger Bands with the actions they indicate.
1. Narrow bands
2. Wide bands
3. Prices rally above the narrow bands.
4. Price fall below the narrow bands.

A. Go long.
B. Go short.
C. Sell options.
D. Buy options.

X

Risk Management

You may have a brilliant trading system — but if your method of money management is clumsy, you will lose money. At some point your system will enter an inevitable drawdown period. If you do not know what to do, you will lose your feeling of control and try to trade your way out of the hole. Losses will snowball and bury your trading account.

On the other hand, when you encounter a losing streak, you may feel disgusted and abandon a perfectly good trading system, giving up large future profits. Either way, a trader is sure to lose without good money management.

Managing money in your trading account is essential for your survival and success as a trader. Professionals spend a lot more time than amateurs thinking about how much money to risk on any trade and how to vary the size of their trades depending on market conditions and their account equity.

Answer the first three questions in this chapter. If you answer fewer than two of them right, please review the recommended reading materials. If you answer two or three questions correctly, proceed to the rest of this chapter. Do not rush, take your time to think. Remember, your money is at stake.

Questions	Trial 1	Trial 2	Trial 3	Trial 4	Trial 5
181					
182					
183					
184					
185					
186					
187					
188					
189					
190					
191					
192					
193					
194					
195					
196					
197					
198					
199					
200					
201					
202					
203					
Correct answers					

Question 181

A trader feels elated when his trading is profitable and disgusted or hurt when a trade goes against him. This means that
   A. he is on the right track; it is important to listen to your feelings
   B. his mind is clouded by emotions and he cannot make good trading decisions
   C. he should double the size of his position when he feels happy and get out when he feels hurt
   D. it does not matter what he feels, as long as his trades are profitable at the end of the day

Question 182

Traders hang onto losing trades for all of these reasons *except*
   A. they become attached to positions
   B. they hate to admit they are wrong
   C. they follow sound trading plans
   D. taking a loss means giving up hope

Question 183

You see an opportunity to make $900 while risking $400. You put on a trade, but the market moves $350 against you. Now is the time to
   A. keep your stop where you put it
   B. take the loss immediately
   C. identify another support level $100 away; a small additional risk to stay in the trade
   D. cancel the stop to avoid getting whipsawed

Question 184

When trading futures, a trader has to deal with

I. the trader's edge
II. the house advantage
III. positive mathematical expectation
IV. negative mathematical expectation

A. I and III
B. II and IV
C. I, II, III, and IV
D. None of the above

Question 185

You go long after an indicator turns up. Two days later, the market slides, that indicator turns down, and you have a $200 paper loss. Your initial stop was $300 below the market, and the next support level is $350 below your entry point. What do you do?

A. Continue to observe the market, keep your stop.
B. Take your loss and retreat to the sidelines.
C. Double up your position; if you're right, you'll come out way ahead, and if you're wrong, the loss on the second half will be small.
D. Lower your stop to slightly below the next logical support level.

Question 186

Your trading system gives a buy signal, which historically has been 70 percent correct. At the same time, another indicator that gives rare signals which are correct 80 percent of the time tells you to trade in the same direction. The likelihood of your making money on this trade is

A. below 70 percent
B. between 70 and 80 percent
C. 80 percent
D. above 80 percent

Question 187

Two traders decide to spend their coffee break flipping a coin and betting 25¢ on each flip. Trader A brings $1 to the game, trader B brings $10. The chance of trader A winning the game is

A. near 100 percent
B. near 50 percent
C. near 0 percent
D. none of the above

Question 188

Choose the order of importance of these three money management goals.
  I. Earn high profits
  II. Ensure survival
  III. Earn a steady rate of return

A. I, II, III
B. II, III, I
C. III, II, I

Question 189

You open a $20,000 trading account to take advantage of a well-researched trading system. You should try to
  I. earn 25 percent profit in a year
  II. lose no more than 25 percent in a year
  III. risk no more than 25 percent on any given trade
  IV. double the size of your trades after making a 25 percent profit

A. I
B. I and II

C. I, II, and III
D. I, II, III, and IV

Question 190

What is the most you may risk on a single trade if your account size is $5000, $25,000, or $100,000?
  A. $50, $250, $1000
  B. $100, $ 500, $2000
  C. $200, $1000, $4000
  D. $500, $2000, $5000

Question 191

You have $16,000 in your trading account when your trading system indicates a very attractive trade. It has great profit potential, while a cutoff point is also clear—if the market goes against you $75 per contract, all bets are off and you should get out. Your broker wants a $2000 margin and $20 commission per contract. You see a great opportunity. How many contracts do you trade?
  A. 1
  B. 3
  C. 5
  D. 7

Question 192

You have traded your account from $20,000 up to $28,000 in six months. Now you are being hit with a string of losses, and your account is down to $24,000. You have "pulled in your horns," reduced the size of your trades, and trade only single contracts. Today your system indicates a trade, with a profit potential of $2000 per contract and risk of $200. You can make up for the the losses of several months in a single trade and get ahead! Required margin—$4000 per contract. How many contracts do you trade?

A. 1

B. 2

C. 4

D. 6

Question 193

Trading the "optimal f"—the optimal fixed fraction of your account—means risking a variable fraction of your capital on each trade, depending on the current performance of your trading system and account size. Which statement regarding trading at the optimal f is *not* correct?

A. If you trade less than the optimal size, your profits decrease geometrically.

B. If you trade less than the optimal size, your risk decreases geometrically.

C. If you risk more than optimal size, you gain no benefit.

D. If you trade double the optimal size, you are virtually certain to go broke.

Question 194

Which of these rules have been proven by computerized testing?

I. Never meet a margin call.

II. Never average down.

III. The first mistake is the cheapest.

IV. If you must lighten up, liquidate your worst position.

A. I

B. I and II

C. I, II, and III

D. I, II, III, and IV

Question 195

The trend is up in soybeans; you go long one contract, and beans rise to a new high. Now you should count
  I. how many ticks beans went up
  II. how many cents beans went up
  III. how many dollars you've made so far
  IV. how much you would have made if you bought two contracts

  A. I
  B. I and II
  C. I, II, and III
  D. I, II, III, and IV

Question 196

You have $25,000 in your account and go long two contracts of gold with a stop $2 away from the market ($200 risk per contract). Gold moves $6 in your favor and indicators point up. You may do any of the following *except*
  A. leave your stop where it is
  B. move your stop to a break-even level
  C. take profits on one contract
  D. buy one more contract

Question 197

When you find yourself counting money in a trade
  I. stop—and if you can't, then close out that trade
  II. use it to calculate your stops
  III. use it to calculate your profit targets
  IV. plot a chart of your account equity

A. I
B. I and II
C. I, II, and III
D. I, II, III, and IV

Question 198

When you plan to exit a trade,
  I. set a stop and exit when it gets hit
  II. have a target before putting on the trade and exit when it gets hit
  III. exit when the indicators that gave you the signals to enter reverse and point in the opposite direction
  IV. exit after a trade goes your way—quit while you're ahead

A. I
B. I and II
C. I, II, and III
D. I, II, III, and IV

Question 199

Which of the following statements about stops are true?
  I. When you are long, do not move stops down.
  II. When you are short, a stop may be moved down.
  III. When you are long, a stop may be moved up.
  IV. When you are short, do not move stops up.

A. I and IV
B. II and III
C. None of the above
D. I, II, III, and IV

Question 200

A stop-loss order
  I. limits your loss on a bad trade
  II. gives you peace of mind
  III. protects you from bad trading systems
  IV. guarantees that your loss will not exceed a certain amount

  A. I
  B. I and II
  C. I, II, and III
  D. I, II, III, and IV

Question 201

Move your stop to a break-even level when
  A. the market closes in your favor
  B. you have $200 or greater paper profit
  C. the Parabolic system tells you to do it
  D. prices move in your favor and away from your entry point by
     more than the average daily range

Question 202

When you adjust protect-profit orders, you may
  I. move your stop so that no more than 2 percent of your account
     equity is exposed
  II. protect 50 percent of your paper profit
  III. use the Parabolic system
  IV. use short-term support and resistance zones

A. I
B. I and II
C. I, II, and III
D. I, II, III, and IV

Question 203

The best way to learn from your trading is to
    I. discuss your trades with acquaintances
    II. keep a diary of your thoughts and feelings about trading
    III. keep a before-and-after chartbook of your trades
    IV. simply keep trading and soaking up the experiences

A. I
B. I and IV
C. II
D. II and III

PART TWO

Answers and Rating Scales

Introduction

Answer 1

C. I and IV. Fundamental analysts analyze economic conditions; technical analysts study market behavior. Both can help you spot good trading opportunities (Section 2).

Answer 2

C. The three pillars of successful trading are sound psychology, good analytic method, and careful money management. A good trader is his own insider (Section 2).

Answer 3

A. The attitude of benign skepticism is the best. Borrow the ideas that seem to make sense and test them in the crucible of your own experience (Section 2).

Answer 4

D. Slippage and commissions slant the "playing field" against most traders; emotional trading finishes them off. Theft is only a minor factor in well-policed markets (Section 3).

Answer 5

D. When the winner receives less than the loser lost, their transaction is called a "minus-sum game." Commissions and slippage make trading a prime example of such a game. Many providers of financial services try to obfuscate this fact (Section 3).

Answer 6

D. To measure the impact of commissions on your trading, compare them to margin. If you make eight trades like this in a year, you will have to earn a 20 percent profit simply to stay even. Slippage can take a bigger cut from your account than commissions and raise the bar to success even higher. Only amateurs neglect the impact of these expenses (Section 3).

Answer 7

B. You lost $0.20/oz buying a 100-oz contract, for a total of $20. You also lost $0.30/oz or $30 per contract in the process of selling, making slippage on the trade $50. This, and commission, has to be added to the $200 loss on the trade itself (Section 3).

Answer 8

C. You lost $200 per trade, plus $25 commission, plus $50 slippage. The winner gained $200, from which he had to pay $25 commission and $50 slippage. Total gain to the trading industry was $150 ($75 + $75)—a whopping 75 percent of the $200 gain. This is why the health of the trading industry depends on an inflow of new losers with new money (Section 3).

Rating Yourself

Fewer than 4 correct   Poor. Take heart—the questions that you've tried to answer are seldom asked. The financial services industry tries hard to conceal many of

	them. Take your time, read the recommended materials, and retake this test.
4–6 correct	Fairly good. You have grasped the basic ideas. Look up the answers to the questions you've missed. Think about them and retake this test in a few days.
7–8 correct	Excellent. You have grasped several important trading concepts. You will enjoy the chapters on psychology and money management.

Recommended Reading

Elder, Alexander. *Trading for a Living* (New York: John Wiley & Sons, 1993). See Introduction.

I

Individual Psychology

Answer 9

D. Trading is inherently risky—traders must deal with the uncertainty of the future. Emotional reactions—fear, elation, hurt—are typical of amateurs. A professional trader measures each risk in advance and trades only when the odds are strongly in his favor (Section 4).

Answer 10

A. You must try to achieve your personal best, to become the best trader you can be. Focusing on money, trading to buy expensive toys, or trying to impress your family makes you take your eyes off the top goal—reaching your personal best. A good surgeon does not count money at the operating table—and neither does an intelligent trader while he is in a trade (Section 4).

Answer 11

C. Nobody likes to look for skeletons in their closet—but you have to learn from your mistakes and find the causes of losses. This needs to be done, even though it is emotionally hard. Trying to trade your way out of a hole, with or without a new guru, is doomed to failure. You need to figure out exactly what got you into the hole in the first place (Section 5).

Answer 12

A. A large account allows you to diversify, to trade multiple contracts, and to spend proportionately less on services. Beginners often discard these advantages by blowing money away simply because it exists in their accounts (Section 5).

Answer 13

D. III and IV. Commercial trading systems are designed to fit old data and self-destruct when markets change. An intelligent trader who develops his own system can make the necessary adjustments; a trader who purchased a system sinks with it. Even systems with built-in optimization do not work because we do not know what kinds of optimization will work in the future. Taking trading signals from any system requires personal discipline and evokes essentially the same emotions as independent trading. There is no substitute for mature judgment (Section 5).

Answer 14

D. Markets move in response to different sets of conditions at different times. Almost any analytic method may eventually come in gear with the market, only to fall out of gear when conditions change. You need to be flexible and use good judgment in order to adjust analytic or trading methods. Few gurus, intoxicated by success, are capable of that (Section 6).

Answer 15

D. The mastery of money management is essential for trading success. You need discipline to cut losses before they cut up your account. Once you accept that, many analytic or trading methods can work well for you (Section 6).

Answer 16

B. II and IV. A trader needs to think for himself. Relying on a guru may bring some profits in the short run, but in the long run it leads to psychological dependence and losses (Section 6).

Answer 17

D. Gambling exists in all societies as a harmless social diversion for those who can stop gambling at will. Gambling can be a career for a cool professional operator. Those who become addicted to the excitement of gambling suffer severe and persistent losses. Quick acquisition of riches is a common delusion among addicted gamblers. Even if they make money at some point, they feel compelled to gamble again and quickly bleed their profits back into the markets (Section 7).

Answer 18

C. I, II, and III. One key sign of a gambling attitude is the inability to stop trading, stay on the sidelines, and reflect on one's behavior. Traders who gamble usually have poor trading results; they often reverse their positions and feel depressed or elated depending on the outcome of their latest trade. If you hit a losing streak, stop trading until you've spent time re-evaluating your method. Serious traders stop to think and learn from their losses, while gamblers continue with their compulsive trading (Section 7).

Answer 19

A. What's the point of nice historical results if the system is destroying your account in the present? To find out what is wrong, start keeping a diary and study your reasons for entering and exiting trades. Pay attention to your feelings while you trade and watch for signs of self-sabotage. Use what you learn to develop a new trading system (Section 7).

Answer 20

C. If your life is a mess, trading will not provide an escape. Personal discipline is essential for trading success. Start looking for common problems in your trading and everyday life. You seem to have serious problems with responsibility. You need to face it and start changing yourself as a person in order to be able to succeed in trading (Section 7).

Answer 21

D. I and IV. Your feelings influence every trade, including your entry, exit, money management, and so on. If your mind is clouded by fear or greed, no system can help you. You do not have to be more intelligent than other traders—only better disciplined. Getting high from trading leads to gambling, accepting bad odds, and losing (Section 8).

Answer 22

C. I and III. You may increase your trading size as long as you do not risk a greater share of your equity than before; a vacation from trading may not be a bad idea—spend some of the time analyzing what you did right. On the other hand, becoming sloppy with stops and lazy in research are typical behaviors of a loser on a lucky streak (Section 8).

Answer 23

B. The next time you see a bumper sticker that says "One day at a time," remember that the car is probably being driven by an AA member. AA's focus on practical results, on staying sober one day at a time, provides a good lesson for traders. It is important to understand what drives one to drink—but the sobriety comes first (Section 9).

Answer 24

D. An alcoholic's life spins out of control—alcohol controls him while he is trying to manage the unmanageable. This is called denial (Section 9).

Answer 25

D. The two key signs of alcoholism are loss of control over drinking and damage to one's life. Being able to suppress drinking on weekdays does not make the problem less real. If anything, this is an example of the self-deception that alcoholics are so good at (Section 9).

Answer 26

A. An alcoholic may not drink alcohol for as long as he lives. He is powerless over alcohol and must struggle to stay sober, day after day. The sooner he recognizes that, the better off he is (Section 9).

Answer 27

D. Losers cannot stop trading in order to think and reflect. They are addicted to the thrill of the game and hope for a big win. They keep poor records, just like alcoholics do not count their drinks. They switch trading systems and methods, just like alcoholics switch from drinking at home to drinking in a bar (Section 10).

Answer 28

C. Losers are hooked on the excitement of trading and keep hoping for a large win. Losers almost always blame their losses on others; not accepting personal responsibility is a sign of a sore amateur (Section 10).

Answer 29

D. Accepting personal responsibility for your losses—past, present, and future—blows away the smoke of illusions and puts your trading on a new, realistic footing. A better trading system, new trading methods, and a major bull market can help, but personal responsibility comes first (Section 10).

Answer 30

B. II and III. A trader who has the courage to recognize his tendency to lose is likely to cut his losses short and avoid overtrading. His discipline frees him from fear, but it does not reduce commissions or slippage—that depends on careful shopping for a broker (Section 10).

Answer 31

C. Staying calm and using your intellect are the cornerstones of successful trading. Bigger capital, knowledgeable friends, the history of success in other endeavors are all desirable—but none equals the importance of a cool and determined intellect.

Emotional trading is the enemy of success. If trading makes you feel giddy or frightens you, those feelings cloud your intelligence. Stop trading when you feel the grip of emotion (Section 11).

Answer 32

D. I, II, III, and IV. Trading provides a tremendous entertainment value. Sure, most traders would like to make money, but even losing provides plenty of thrills. Some enjoy the intellectual challenge of the game and spend years at it. The nonfinancial rewards must be high, especially since some 90 percent of traders lose money (Section 11).

Answer 33

A. If your own emotions make you jump in and out of trades, you're trading with a clouded mind. If your trading is under the control of your emotions, then the market must appear illogical to you. Other problems, such as a shortage of good information, small capital, or a degree of randomness in the markets, are relatively minor causes of traders' confusion, compared to emotional trading (Section 11).

Answer 34

D. Only a fearful trader grabs the bulk of profits from his account. A winner has a trading system and a money management plan. He is in no hurry to get rich, and he stops to think after victories and defeats. He treats trading as a business—and few businessmen siphon the bulk of profits from a well-established enterprise (Section 11).

Answer 35

C. A trade begins only when you decide to enter the market and ends only when you decide to exit. Those decisions are yours alone—and if you let others decide for you, you'll be a loser. You may use technical indicators, rely on fundamental analysis, or even pay attention to trusted advisors—but only you can decide when a trade begins and when it ends (Section 11).

Rating Yourself

Fewer than 7 correct	Poor. The red light is flashing—your level of understanding puts you in danger. You need to learn more about trading psychology in order to have the chance of succeeding as a trader. Many psychological tricks that help people get by in their daily lives destroy them in the markets. Our educational system promotes dependence and follow-the-leader mentality. Successful traders are independent, creative, and realistic. Please study the recommended reading materials and retake this test before proceeding to the rest of this book.
7–15 correct	Below average. Getting half the answers right (being in the bottom half) is not good enough since more than half of all traders lose money and wash out of the markets. You need to learn more about the individual psychology of trading. Study the issues of reality versus fantasy, dealing with self-destructiveness, and the differences in the thinking of winners and losers. Please reread the relevant materials and retake this test.
16–22 correct	Fairly good. You have a working grasp of the essential concepts of trading psychology but

need to fill in the gaps. Please read the recommended literature and retake this test a few days later. Good traders never stop analyzing the markets and their own reactions to them.

Over 22 correct   Excellent. You have mastered the topics in this chapter. Please review those questions where your answers differed from those provided in this book. All successful traders have a high degree of independence. See whether the discrepancies were due to errors—or to your own, individual way of thinking.

Recommended Reading

Elder, Alexander. *Trading for a Living* (New York: John Wiley & Sons, 1993). See Chapter I, "Individual Psychology."

Additional Reading

Douglas, Mark. *The Disciplined Trader* (New York: New York Institute of Finance, 1990).
Lefevre, Edwin. *Reminiscences of a Stock Operator* (1923). (Greenville, SC: Traders Press, 1985).

II

Mass Psychology

Answer 36

D. Price is whatever the crowd of traders says it is at any given moment. Prices reflect reality, as seen by masses of market participants. Prices are established by crowds of those who make buy and sell decisions. "Supply and demand curves" are far removed from the sweaty reality of the market crowd. Prices are connected to fundamental values in the long run but are governed by crowd psychology from day to day (Section 12).

Answer 37

D. Bulls try to buy low, bears try to sell high, and both know they have to hurry before some undecided trader steps in and snatches a trade away from them. The goal of a good technical analyst is to discover the balance of power between bulls and bears and bet on the winning group. Professionals trade with the dominant market group, while beginners try to forecast the future (Section 12).

Answer 38

B. When you trade, you try to rob others while they are trying to rob you. Thinking of this crowd as some electronic signal removes you from its sweaty reality. All members of the market crowd are swayed by the currents of greed and fear, further reducing their ability to make rational decisions. There is no free money at this carnival (Section 13).

Answer 39

A. "When in doubt, stay out" is a good old trading rule. Most traders cannot stay away from the game. They read newspapers and newsletters, watch TV, listen to gossip, and jump into the markets. Why trade, whether a large or a small size, when you are not sure what to do? (Section 13).

Answer 40

C. Any profits you make have to come from other traders. Make sure to guard your own pockets, because other traders will try to pick them before you can pick theirs. Brokers and exchanges will take a cut from you, whether you win, lose, or draw (Section 13).

Answer 41

D. I, II, III, and IV. Trading on inside information is illegal in the U.S. stock and options markets but legal in most of the world. Having inside information does not guarantee success. If you use it, you need to know how to act on it, which is why many of the alleged "insider tips" lead to losses. Many amateurs are surprised to find out that trading on many kinds of inside information is legal in the futures markets (Section 13).

Answer 42

C. Institutional traders are well capitalized, some are well trained, and many have access to inside information and good research (not that they always use it). The individual trader has one great advantage—flexibility. He can wait for the best opportunities—he does not have to trade daily, like most institutional traders. Most individuals fritter away this advantage by not waiting for the trades with the best odds of success (Section 14).

Answer 43

D. I, II, III, and IV. An average private trader is a 50-year-old college-educated male. The two largest professional groups among private traders are farmers and engineers. They enjoy the challenge of the game but keep losing money. Unlike institutional traders, they have no bosses to limit their losses (Section 14).

Answer 44

A. I and II. Some newsletters can provide interesting trading ideas and are fun to read. Letter writers are theoreticians—few if any are trading experts. They usually go through hot and cold periods, and if you apply yourself to analysis and trading you will soon know more about trading than most letter writers (Section 14).

Answer 45

B. I and III. When people join crowds, they become more emotional and short-term oriented. Their impulsive behavior leads to a great deal of volatility in the financial markets. Crowd members trust leaders more than themselves. Their psychological dependence makes them unwilling or unable to leave the crowd, until they are shaken by a severe loss (Section 15).

Answer 46

D. I, II, III, and IV. The greater the uncertainty, the more people tend to look up to others for reassurance. This behavior is deeply ingrained in human nature. Loyalty of members to the leader holds crowds together. A leader may be an individual, an idea, or, in the case of the financial markets, price itself (Section 15).

Answer 47

A. I. Crowds are bigger and stronger than you; do not argue with the market. You can exploit the primitive and repetitive behavior of market crowds by using simple strategies. Market crowds are often right during trends but wrong at the turning points. When you let the market make you feel elated or depressed, you lose your independence; professional traders stay cool (Section 15).

Answer 48

C. Almost all eyes in the market are glued to prices. The longer a rally lasts, the more bulls it brings out, and the longer a decline persists, the more bears join the party. This is why market moves perpetuate themselves. Few financial firms are big enough to dominate a large market for a few days or even hours. Gurus are to the market as a tail is to a dog—few dogs chase their tail for very long. Fundamental changes in the economy create conditions for bull and bear markets, but only traders can buy, sell, and create trends (Section 15).

Answer 49

B. II and III. Every change in price reflects what happens in the battle between bulls and bears. Markets rise when bulls feel more strongly than bears. They rally when buyers are confident and sellers demand a premium for participating in the game that is going against them. There is a buyer and a seller behind every transaction. The number of stocks or futures bought and sold is equal by definition (Section 16).

Answer 50

D. I, II, III, and IV. When the trend is down, shorts who are winning want to add to their positions. They are willing to sell at a discount, confident that the downtrend will make money for them. At the same time, bulls who are losing feel disgusted and get out. They are in no hurry to buy and place their bids below the market, forcing bears to sell cheaper and cheaper. This process is reversed during uptrends (Section 16).

Answer 51

B. II and III. A price shock is a sudden move against the trend. It frightens the dominant group and makes the opposition feel bolder. A sudden price break in an uptrend provides a price shock that frightens the bulls. Even if they manage to take prices to a new high, their confidence is shaken, and the uptrend is ready for a reversal (Section 16).

Answer 52

C. A bearish divergence occurs when prices rally to a new high while an indicator rises to a lower peak. In a bullish divergence, prices fall to a new low while an indicator falls to a more shallow low. Bearish divergences occur during uptrends and help identify tops. Bullish divergences occur during downtrends and help identify market bottoms. These are among the most useful patterns in technical analysis (Section 16).

Answer 53

1. B; 2. C; 3. A; 4. D. Fundamental analysts study economic factors, technical analysts study price changes. Some good traders know how to combine both. The illusion of becoming an insider from watching famous analysts does not alter the reality of being a hunch player (Section 17).

Answer 54

C. I, II, and III. Technical analysis is a study of past prices. It involves objective scientific methods but it also requires a degree of artistic flair and being able to see the whole behind the clutter of the elements. Technical analysis provides ample opportunities to deceive yourself into seeing what you want. If someone tells you it is a simple skill, hold on to your wallet (Section 17).

Answer 55

B. I and IV. An analyst must stay calm, focus on the reality of the market, identify the current trend, and get in gear with it. When traders try to forecast, their egos get wedded to their predictions. It becomes hard for them to change their trading stance when the market refuses to follow a forecast—and they get financially hurt (Section 17).

Rating Yourself

Fewer than 6 correct   Poor. You have a very limited understanding of mass psychology of the markets. If you do not know how the market crowds behave and how they influence your mind, you are like a piece of driftwood floating on the waves. Please study the recommended reading materials and retake this test in a few days, before proceeding to the rest of this book.

6–10 correct   Below average. You do not understand the markets well enough. You need to learn more about the psychological balance between bulls and bears, the impact of the trading crowds on you, and the difference between managing trades and forecasting prices. Please study the relevant materials and retake this test.

11–15 correct   Fairly good. You have a working grasp of the essential concepts of mass psychology, but need to know more. Remember, the time to think about mass psychology is now, not when the markets buffet your open position. Please read the recommended reading materials and retake this test in a few days. Continue to monitor the impact of the market crowd on you when you trade.

Over 15 correct   Excellent. You have mastered the essential concepts in this chapter. Now review some of your recent trades in light of these principles and continue to monitor the impact of the market crowd as you trade. As you move on to the chapters on market analysis, keep in mind that technical analysis is applied social psychology.

Recommended Reading

Elder, Alexander. *Trading for a Living* (New York: John Wiley & Sons, 1993). See Chapter II, "Mass Psychology."

Additional Reading

LeBon, Gustave. *The Crowd* (1897). (Atlanta, GA: Cherokee Publishing, 1982). Mackay, Charles. *Extraordinary Popular Delusions and the Madness of Crowds* (1841). (New York: Crown Publishers, 1980).

III

Classical Chart Analysis

Answer 56

1–D; 2–C; 3–A; 4–B. Amateurs usually get their information at night and trade in the morning. Professionals respond to changing conditions throughout the day and often dominate the market at closing time. Buying pushes prices up, and the highest price of the day marks the maximum power of bulls. Selling pushes prices down, and the lowest price of the day marks the maximum power of bears. This reasoning also applies to weekly and intraday charts (Section 18).

Answer 57

D. I, II, III, and IV. Wishful thinking is rampant among analysts, especially those who do not trade. A measure of arrogance is actually useful when trying to sell advisory services to traders. Keeping basic definitions fuzzy contributes to the confusion (Section 18).

Answer 58

C. Slippage tends to be lower during quiet, narrow-range days. Narrow ranges enable you to use tighter stops, reducing your financial risk. Commissions do not depend on volatility (Section 18).

Answer 59

B. The horizontal line B, drawn across the January and March bottoms, marks the area of support. The horizontal line C started out as resistance but changed to support after prices rallied above it. Support and resistance frequently reverse their roles: The area of resistance on the way up often becomes the area of support on the way down, and vice versa. The diagonal lines A and D are a downtrendline and an uptrendline, respectively (Section 19).

Answer 60

D. I and IV. Support and resistance lines are drawn across either the highs or the lows. The edges of congestion areas show where masses of traders have traded and reversed their positions. Extreme prices show only the levels of panic among the weakest bulls and bears (Section 19).

Answer 61

D. I, II, III, and IV. Support and resistance exist because traders have memories. The more intense their memories, the more prone they are to buy and sell, and the stronger the support and resistance. High volume shows greater financial and emotional commitment, as does the height of the support and resistance zone. The more time prices have spent in a congestion area and the more times that area has been hit, the more traders expect a new reversal to occur and act accordingly (Section 19).

Answer 62

C. I, II, and III. Waiting for a new low helps to ensure that you are dealing with a downside breakout. A false breakout is the bane of amateurs, but professional traders love them. They often wait until a downside breakout stops making new lows and then trade against it, placing a protective stop at the latest low (Section 19).

Answer 63

C. At point 2 heating oil is rallying into resistance. Depending on how bullish or how cautious you are, it may pay to tighten your stops, take profits, or even leave the stop where it is. It is seldom a good idea to add to longs when prices are hitting resistance. It is safer to buy after the resistance has been penetrated. Two pullbacks in April offered two good buying opportunities (Section 19).

Answer 64

1. D; 2. C; 3. A; 4. B. A downtrendline connects the tops of rallies in a downtrend. An uptrendline connects the bottoms of declines in an uptrend. The area between support C and resistance B is a trading range (Section 20).

Answer 65

Trends—A, D, and E; Trading ranges—B, C, and F. A trend exists when prices keep rising or falling over time, reaching higher highs or lower lows. In trading ranges, most rallies peter out at approximately the same highs and declines stop at approximately the same lows. As a trader, when you recognize a trend, follow it and try to hang onto positions. On the other hand, if you trade the swings within a trading range, be extra careful not to overstay your position (Section 20).

Answer 66

1. D; 2. C; 3. B; 4. A. Go long when prices are in the vicinity of the rising trendline, especially when daily ranges are narrow. As soon as you buy, place a protective stop slightly below the trend-line; move it up to protect your profits when prices rally. A wide-range day closing near the lows shows that bears are strong and the uptrendline may be breaking (Section 20).

Answer 67

C. I, II, and III. The trend is your friend. As long as you see the pattern of higher highs and higher lows, trade that market from the long side. Make sure to protect your position with stops and move them up as the trend progresses. Add to your positions only after your paper profits have been protected. If the market takes out its previous low, it throws the uptrend in doubt (Section 20).

Answer 68

B. The edges of congestion areas show where the majority of traders have reversed direction. Bottoms of declines show where bears stopped and bulls regained control of the market. The extreme lows show only the capacity for panic among the weak-est bulls. How long a trendline remains inviolate, or how many times prices touch it, becomes clear only after the fact. Meanwhile, we need to draw our trendlines as early as possible (Section 21).

Answer 69

A. Tails show that either a high or a low price level has been rejected by the mass of market participants. Since markets con-stantly fluctuate, it pays to trade in the direction opposite a tail. You can identify several tails on this chart, followed by reversals. When a market starts "chewing its tail," moving back into its tail area, it is time to reverse a position (Section 21).

Answer 70

C. III, IV, I, II. The single most important feature of a trendline is the direction of its slope. When a trendline slants up, it shows that bulls are in control—it is time to trade from the long side. When a trendline slants down, it shows that bears are in control and tells you to trade from the short side. The longer a trendline persists, the greater the inertia of the dominant market crowd. The number of contacts reinforces the validity of a trendline, as does expanding volume when prices move away from their trendline (Section 21).

Answer 71

A. When prices break an uptrendline and then pull back to it from below, they almost always offer a good shorting opportunity, with a close stop slightly above the trendline. Breaking of a trendline does not necessarily signal the death of an uptrend; it depends on the margin of the penetration, the pattern of a longer-term chart, and the signals of technical indicators. Stops must be kept very tight during vertical price moves; if prices rally straight up, they can also come crashing down (Section 21).

Answer 72

1. A; 2. D; 3. B; 4. C; 5. C–D. Common gaps occur in the midst of congestion areas. Continuation gaps occur in the midst of trends. Breakaway gaps occur when prices break out of congestion areas. When prices refuse to reach new highs after gapping up or new lows after gapping down, you are probably dealing with an exhaustion gap. An island reversal is a pattern that starts as an exhaustion gap, followed by a compact trading area and then a breakaway gap in the opposite direction of the preceding trend (Section 22).

Answer 73

D. I, II, III, and IV. Gaps occur when prices open outside of the previous day's range and stay there all day. Gaps occur when masses of traders get shocked by a news development; other gaps reflect changing prices in the overseas markets while the local exchange was closed. When floor traders detect a strong imbalance of buy and sell orders prior to the opening, they open that market sharply higher or lower (Section 22).

Answer 74

1. B; 2. A; 3. A; 4. C. Common gaps do not provide good trading signals and are best ignored. If you must trade, fade them (trade against them). When you identify an upside breakaway or a continuation gap, go long. Go short when you identify an upside exhaustion gap. It may be safer to buy put options, due to the higher volatility at many tops. Waiting for a pullback is usually a poor tactic when dealing with gaps (Section 22).

Answer 75

1. C; 2. D; 3. B; 4. A. The left and right shoulders are formed by rally peaks. They surround the head—a higher peak. A neckline is drawn across the bottoms of declines from the left and right shoulders. A downsloping neckline is especially bearish (Section 23).

Answer 76

C. I, II, and III. If you go short while the right shoulder is being formed, place a protective stop slightly above the top of the head. Make it a stop-and-reverse order—not only should you cover shorts, you should also go long if the head-and-shoulders pattern is aborted. When prices break the neckline and then pull back to it from below, they offer an excellent shorting opportunity, with a tight protective stop slightly above the neckline. Once you go short in a downtrend, hang onto your position—do not cover simply because prices are near short-term support. Too many traders feel demoralized by previous losses and grab the first small profit that comes their way (Section 23).

Answer 77

B. The top of the head is near 13.50, while the neckline is at approximately 12.00 at point X—a distance of approximately 1.50. Project this distance down from the break of the neckline, near 11.80. 11.80 – 1.50 = 10.30. It is reasonable to expect cocoa to slide to that area or lower (Section 23).

Answer 78

A. T and R; B. T; C. T; D. R. The upper boundaries of triangles and rectangles mark areas of resistance, while their lower boundaries mark areas of support. These lines are parallel in rectangles but converge in triangles. Breakouts from the first half of a triangle are more likely to result in a strong price trend. The opposite is true in rectangles—the longer they last, the greater the move after the breakout (Section 23).

Answer 79

1. E; 2. A, B; 3. D; 4. C. The upper and lower boundaries of a symmetrical triangle converge at the same angles. An ascending triangle has a relatively flat upper boundary and a rising lower boundary. A descending triangle has a relatively flat lower boundary, but its upper boundary slants down. The upper and lower lines of a rectangle are parallel and horizontal. Notice how the area of resistance on the way up—the upper line of rectangle C—became support on the way down—the lower line of the triangle D (Section 23).

Answer 80

C. I, II, and III. When the trend is up, most tactics for going long make sense. The choice depends on your degree of bullishness and account size. Whatever you do, keep your protective sell orders on long positions. Trading without stops is dangerous. If you go long inside a triangle, place a protective stop immediately below that triangle. If you go long on a breakout or on a pullback, place a protective stop within the triangle, immediately below its upper boundary (Section 23).

Rating Yourself

Fewer than 7 correct	Poor. Charts tell an important story—and if you cannot read them, you will miss their message. You run a serious risk of buying at the tops and selling at the bottoms. Please study the recommended reading materials, review your charts, apply the lessons you've learned, and then retake this test. Do not proceed to the next chapter until then—these materials are too important to skip.
7–13 correct	Below average. You have a slim chance of winning the trading game. All serious investors and traders need to grasp such essential concepts as trends and trading ranges, support and resistance, continuation and reversal. Please review the recommended reading materials and retake this test.
14–20 correct	Fairly good. You have a working knowledge of the key concepts of charting. Now you have to

decide whether "fairly good" is good enough for you. It may be enough if you plan to focus on computerized technical analysis, but not enough if you plan to work with charts. In that case, please return to the recommended reading materials and learn to recognize and interpret gaps, trendlines, triangles, heads and shoulders, and other patterns. Then retake this test.

Over 20 correct — Excellent. You have mastered the essential concepts of charting. They can help you discover the shifts of power between bulls and bears. Now proceed to the chapters on computerized technical analysis.

Recommended Reading

Elder, Alexander. *Trading for a Living* (New York: John Wiley & Sons, 1993). See Chapter III, "Classical Chart Analysis."

Additional Reading

Edwards, Robert D., and John Magee. *Technical Analysis of Stock Trends* (1948). (New York: New York Institute of Finance, 1992).
Pring, Martin J. *Technical Analysis Explained,* 3rd edition (New York: McGraw-Hill, 1991).

IV

Computerized Technical Analysis

Answer 81

A. I. Computerized technical analysis is more objective than classical charting. You may argue whether a triangle is present or not, but there can be no argument about the direction of an indicator—it is either up or down. A good technician tries to discover the balance of power between bulls and bears and bet on the winning group—not to forecast the future. A computer does not remove all emotions from trading—the order to buy or sell still has to be placed by the individual. As for the "sure thing," if anyone tries to sell it to you, beware of a scam (Section 24).

Answer 82

B. Software is the key part of the package. It determines what you see on your screen and what indicators and studies are available to you. Different programs run on different machines, which is why it is better to buy a computer after you choose your software. Most analytic programs read data in many formats, and there are many utility programs for converting data into formats readable by almost any software package (Section 24).

Answer 83

1. C; 2. A; 3. B. A toolbox is a collection of tools. It is useful for a craftsman but can be dangerous in the hands of an amateur.

Black boxes come with excellent historical records but self-destruct when markets change; gray boxes straddle the fence between those two groups (Section 24).

Answer 84

1. C; 2. A; 3. B. To be a successful trader, you must combine indicators from different groups so that their negative features cancel each other out while their positive features remain undisturbed. The Triple Screen trading system has been designed for this purpose (Section 24).

Answer 85

B. To calculate a simple moving average, add the closing prices in its window and divide them by the number of days in that window. Adding prices for the past 5 days produces 110, and dividing 110 by 5 is 22 (Section 25).

Answer 86

A. Exponential moving averages are harder to calculate by hand than simple MAs. If you use a computer, both are equally easy (Section 25).

Answer 87

D. When the EMA rises, it shows that bulls are in control—it is time to go long. When it falls, it shows that bears are in control—it is time to go short. The ability of an EMA to reach a new high or a new low is also important, but much less so than the direction of its slope. The width of its time window is set by the trader (Section 25).

Answer 88

1. A, C; 2. B; 3. A, C; 4. B. When the EMA rises, trade the market only from the long side—place your buy orders slightly below the EMA. When the EMA turns down, trade the market from the short side by placing sell orders slightly above the falling EMA (Section 25).

Answer 89

A. 1, 2, 3, 8; B. 4, 5; C. 6, 7. When the EMA points up, prices usually hover above it and every decline offers a good buying opportunity. When the EMA points down, prices are usually below it and rallies offer good shorting opportunities. The transitional zones between uptrends and downtrends are the hardest to trade. If in doubt, stand aside until a clear trend emerges (Section 25).

Answer 90

D. I, II, III, and IV. Each price is a momentary consensus of value, while a moving average shows the average consensus of value. A shorter-term MA tracks short-term consensus, and a longer-term MA tracks longer-term consensus. When the fast line of MACD is above or below the slow line, it shows whether bulls or bears currently dominate the market (Section 26).

Answer 91

C. MACD-Histogram tracks the spread between the fast and slow MACD lines. Its slope is defined by the relationship between the last two bars of MACD-Histogram. When the slope rises, it shows that bulls are in control, and when it declines, it shows that bears are in control. It pays to trade in the direction of the dominant market group. This is not forecasting—merely betting on the inertia of the market crowd (Section 26).

Answer 92

1. A; 2. C; 3. B; 4. D. When MACD-Histogram reaches a new high, it tells you that bulls are strong and prices are likely to retest or exceed their latest peak. When it falls to a new low, it shows that bears are strong and prices are likely to retest or exceed the latest low. A bullish divergence gives a strong buy signal; it occurs when prices fall to a new low but MACD-Histogram traces a more shallow bottom. A bearish divergence gives a strong sell signal; it occurs when prices rise to a new high but MACD-Histogram traces a lower high. Why not buy at the bottom between areas C and D? Experience has shown that massive tops and bottoms in MACD-Histogram, such as the one in area C, have to be retested twice to create a tradable divergence (Section 26).

Answer 93

C. At this point, a new peak in MACD-Histogram is telling us to expect a higher peak in wheat. The tactic is to remain on the sidelines, using any pullback as a buying opportunity (Section 26).

Answer 94

C. The part of today's bar that protrudes above or below yesterday's bar represents today's directional movement. If today's bar extends both above and below yesterday's bar, then only the longer part represents directional movement. If today's bar does not extend outside yesterday's bar, or if it extends above and below by equal amounts, directional movement is zero (Section 27).

Answer 95

1. D; 2. B; 3. C; 4. A. Trade in the direction of the upper Directional Line as long as ADX rises above the lower Directional Line. When ADX is below both +DI and −DI, avoid using a trend-following method. On this chart of platinum, go short after ADX penetrates above +DI. Cover shorts when ADX turns down from above both Directional Lines (Section 27).

Answer 96

D. III and IV. When ADX falls below both Directional Lines, it does not suggest either buying or selling. The prices, though, are trending higher. It is not uncommon for ADX to take a month or longer to generate a new signal after catching a trend, as it did in platinum in December. It is a good idea to consult other indicators (Section 27).

Answer 97

A. Oscillators measure the speed of market moves. Their peaks and valleys can identify the turning points in mass optimism and pessimism. Overbought readings of oscillators help identify market tops, and oversold readings help catch market bottoms. These signals tend to work during trading ranges but are often premature and dangerous when the market begins to trend. No indicator can catch all tops and bottoms (Section 28).

Answer 98

1. C; 2. B; 3. D; 4. A. Overbought means too high, ready to turn down. Oversold means too low, ready to turn up. Upper and lower reference lines should be drawn so that an oscillator spends only about 5 percent of its time beyond each line (Section 28).

Answer 99

D. When an oscillator reaches a new high, it indicates strength and tells traders that the rally is likely to continue. You may add to long positions or take partial profits, but it is better to ignore shorting signals because under those conditions prices are not likely to drop (Section 28).

Answer 100

A. I and II. When the market trend is down and an oscillator rises above its upper reference line, it identifies a short-term splash of bullishness—a shorting opportunity. Afterward, you may want to cover shorts when momentum falls below its lower reference line or you may want to hold shorts. In any case, do not go long in a well-established downtrend. As Peter Lynch, a noted money manager, once wrote: "Trying to catch a bottom is like trying to catch a falling knife—you invariably grab it in the wrong spot" (Section 28).

Answer 101

1. B; 2. A; 3. D; 4. C; 5. F; 6. E. Class A divergences almost always give good trading signals. Buy when an indicator turns up from the second bottom of a bullish divergence or turns down from the second top of a bearish divergence. Class B divergences give less reliable signals—check the messages of other indicators. Class C divergences are best ignored by traders (Section 28).

Answer 102

C. Wm%R measures the placement of each closing price in relation to the recent high-low range. It expresses the distance from the highest high to the lowest low as 100 percent. It expresses the distance from the latest closing price to the top of that range as a percentage of the range (Section 29).

Answer 103

1. B, D; 2. C, F; 3. H; 4. E, G; 5. A. An oscillator becomes overbought when it rises above its upper reference line. An overbought oscillator gives a signal to sell or at least to avoid buying. An oscillator becomes oversold when it falls below its lower reference line. It gives a signal to buy or at least to avoid shorting. A failure swing occurs when an oscillator fails to reach its reference line during a market move. When Wm%R could not reach its lower reference line during decline A, that failure swing indicated bulls were strong and gave a buy signal. Bullish and bearish divergences provide the strongest buy and sell signals. Bearish divergence G is a Class A divergence, while divergences E and H are Class B divergences (Section 29).

Answer 104

D. All four statements are correct, but their conflicting messages cancel each other out. There is no reason to jump into the market when the trading picture is unclear. Stay on the sidelines and wait for better signals to emerge. If sugar reaches a new high and Wm%R remains below its upper reference line, it will create a Class A bearish divergence and give a strong sell signal. If sugar declines and Wm%R touches its lower reference line, it will give a strong signal to buy, especially since the overall trend is up (Section 29).

Answer 105

C. II and IV. Ideally, tune your Stochastic into the dominant market cycle. If no cycle is present or is hard to find, make your

Stochastic shorter. A shorter window helps Stochastic accomplish its goal—find short-term tops and bottoms (Section 30).

Answer 106

1. C; 2. B; 3. D; 4. A. Each price represents the consensus of value among the mass of market participants at the moment of the trade. The high and the low for the recent time period represent the maximum power of bulls and bears during that time. Stochastic measures the capacity of bulls or bears to close the market near the upper or lower edge of the recent trading range (Section 30).

Answer 107

1. B, I; 2. D, F, H, J; 3. J–K; 4. B–C; 5. A, E, G. Stochastic becomes overbought when it rises to or above its upper reference line. It gives a signal to sell or at least to avoid buying. Stochastic becomes oversold when it falls to or below its lower reference line. It gives a signal to buy or at least to avoid shorting. A failure swing occurs when Stochastic fails to reach its reference line during a market move. When Stochastic could not reach its lower reference line during decline A, it showed that bulls were strong and gave a buy signal. When Stochastic could not reach its upper reference line during rallies E and G, it showed that bears were strong and gave sell signals. Bullish and bearish divergences between Stochastic and prices give the strongest buy and sell signals of this indicator. B–C was a Class A bearish divergence—prices rallied to a new high, while Stochastic traced a lower peak. J–K was a Class A bullish divergence—prices fell to a new low, while Stochastic held above its reference line (Section 30).

Answer 108

B. Considering the fact that Stochastic is rising from a bullish divergence J–K, we can expect the stock to continue to rally. The breakout by Stochastic to a new high for the month is also bullish. Go long and place a protective stop at the level of the latest low, four days prior to the last trading day (Section 30).

Answer 109

B. I and II. Most trading accounts get "pegged to the market" after the close. As a result, closing prices determine the value of trading accounts. Some traders can withdraw money from their accounts, while others receive margin calls, based on closing prices. Few savvy traders "get stuck" with their positions overnight. With more and more markets opening around the world, it is often possible to get out of one's position in the overseas markets (Section 31).

Answer 110

1. A, G, H, K, M; 2. C, D, L, O; 3. D–F; 4. A–B, M–N; 5. E, I. RSI becomes overbought when it rises above its upper reference line. It gives sell signals, which help traders sell short in downtrends or in flat markets but are often premature during uptrends. RSI becomes oversold when it falls below its lower reference line. It gives buy signals, which help traders go long in uptrends or in flat markets but are often premature during downtrends. Bullish and bearish divergences give the strongest buy and sell signals. Two bearish divergences, A–B and M–N, as well as the bullish divergence D–F, are all class A divergences. All three gave their signals prior to substantial market moves (Section 31).

Answer 111

D. I and IV. RSI is based exclusively on changes in closing prices. It often breaks its trendline a few days ahead of prices, telling traders to get ready for a possible change of trend. These breaks give especially strong messages when accompanied by other signals. Notice in Figure 14 how the breaking of a downtrendline E was followed by a bullish divergence D–F, auguring a powerful upmove (Section 31).

Answer 112

A. The downtrend is intact, RSI has fallen to a new low (no bullish divergence), and its downtrendline is unbroken. If you shorted gold after a bearish divergence M–N, continue to hold shorts or take partial profits. It is too risky to initiate short positions when RSI is deeply oversold, and it is too early to go long (Section 31).

Rating Yourself

Fewer than 9 correct	Poor. You have a very limited understanding of modern technical analysis. Whether you plan to use a computer or not, you owe it to yourself to learn the essential concepts. Please study the recommended literature and retake this test.
9–17 correct	Below average. You need to understand the messages of trend-following indicators and oscillators. They offer insights into the balance of power between market bulls and bears. Please study the recommended reading materials and retake this test before proceeding to the rest of this book.
18–24 correct	Fairly good. You have a decent grasp of the essential concepts of computerized technical analysis. Now review your answers to find out your areas of strength and weakness. Are you more comfortable with trend-following indicators or oscillators? Are you better at finding signals that identify trends or reversals? Please

review the recommended literature and retake this test several days later. Think about what these tests reveal about your preferences. Most successful traders concentrate on just a few types of trades. Some prefer to follow trends, while others are better off at catching reversals. Trader, know thyself.

Over 24 correct — Excellent. You have a good command of computerized technical analysis. These indicators are the building blocks of several good trading systems (see Chapter 9). Before we work on a system, let us review other types of indicators available to market analysts (Chapters 5–8).

Recommended Reading

Elder, Alexander. *Trading for a Living* (New York: John Wiley & Sons, 1993). See Chapter IV, "Computerized Technical Analysis."

Additional Reading

Murphy, John J. *Technical Analysis of the Futures Markets* (New York: New York Institute of Finance, 1986).

V

The Neglected Essentials

Answer 113

D. I, II, III, and IV. There are three ways to measure volume: the number of contracts or shares traded, the number of trades, and the number of price changes. The first method provides the most accurate reflection of market activity (Section 32).

Answer 114

A. Each trade represents a financial and emotional commitment by two traders. Since one of them is bound to be wrong, volume reflects the activity of winners and losers. Volume surges when losers panic. It reflects present activity but does not forecast the future (Section 32).

Answer 115

1. B; 2. A; 3. C; 4. D. Trends usually persist when volume is steady or slightly higher. They usually expire with a bang or a whimper—a burst or a drastic shrinkage of volume. The trend cannot continue after losers quit the market (Section 32).

Answer 116

1. D; 2. F; 3. C; 4. A; 5. B, G. Rising or steady volume confirms trends. When prices rise to a new high or fall to a new low while volume shrinks, the trend is likely to reverse. A climactic increase in volume shows that the move has become unsustainable and the market is likely to turn (Section 32).

Answer 117

D. When signals are mixed, as they are now, it pays to stand aside. Wait to trade until you get a clear signal! The markets will be there tomorrow. Winners wait for the best trading opportunities, while amateurs rush to trade for sheer excitement (Section 32).

Answer 118

C. I, II, and III. OBV is created by adding a day's volume to a running total when a trading vehicle rises and subtracting a day's volume from the total when that vehicle declines. OBV confirms bull moves when it rises to a new high; it confirms declines when it falls to new lows. Prices represent the consensus of value, while volume, measured by OBV, tracks traders' emotions (Section 33).

Answer 119

1. B; 2. C, D, E; 3. A. When OBV rose to a new high A, it told traders to expect higher prices ahead. When the stock rose to a new high B, OBV traced a lower peak—a Class A bearish divergence, a good shorting opportunity. OBV led the stock on its way down. Its breakdown at point E gave an especially useful signal—it told traders to hang onto their shorts. The stock was flat for over a month but then followed OBV and renewed its slide (Section 33).

Answer 120

A. The trend of prices is down; the trend of OBV is down. Go short, do not argue with the trend. The fact that OBV has not reached a new low on the last trading day is not cause for alarm.

Important divergences take many days or weeks to develop. The fact that OBV is scraping bottom, hovering right at its lows, is bearish enough (Section 33).

Answer 121

1. D; 2. C; 3. B; 4. A. Opening and closing prices are among the most important prices of the day. Openings are largely dominated by amateurs who crowd into the markets in the mornings. Closings tend to be dominated by market professionals who monitor the conditions all day. Accumulation/Distribution is an indicator that ties volume to the relationship between opening and closing prices (Section 33).

Answer 122

B. Open interest reflects the number of contracts held by longs or owed by shorts in a given market on a given day. Open interest equals either total long or total short position (Section 34).

Answer 123

1. B; 2. C; 3. C; 4. A. Open interest rises only when a new buyer and a new seller enter the market—their trade creates a new contract. Open interest falls when a trader who is long sells to another who is short, because both close out their positions. If a new bull buys from an old bull who is getting out, open interest remains unchanged. Nor does it change when a new bear sells to an old bear who buys to get out of his short position (Section 34).

Answer 124

D. I, II, III, and IV. A rise in the open interest shows that a crowd of confident bulls is facing down a crowd of equally confident bears. One group is sure to lose, but as long as potential losers keep pouring in, the trend is likely to continue (Section 34).

Answer 125

1. C, D; 2. B; 3. A, F; 4. D–E. Rising open interest shows a growing conflict between bulls and bears and confirms the uptrend. Falling open interest shows that bulls are bailing out while bears are taking profits, showing little confidence in the downtrend. When prices rise to a new high but open interest shrinks, it shows that bulls, while victorious, are losing confidence. This is a Class A bearish divergence—go short (Section 34).

Answer 126

D. III and IV. The trend is your friend—do not argue with it. If you had to make a trade on the last day of this chart, you'd have to go short, since the trend is down. Since no one is forcing you to trade, stand aside. The downtrend is old, it is declining into support, and it is risky to go short at this stage. Get ready to sell short into the next minor rally, with a tight stop. If the downtrend reverses and corn rallies above its earlier April top, your stop will be close to the market and you'll be able to reverse and go long (Section 34).

Answer 127

C. I, II, and III. HPI uses daily high and low prices, volume and open interest. HPI confirms valid trends and helps catch their reversals (Section 35).

Answer 128

1. C; 2. B; 3. A; 4. D, E. New highs of HPI confirm price uptrends and new lows of HPI confirm downtrends. Bullish and bearish divergences of HPI often precede trend reversals but have long lead times. Both divergences on this chart are Class A divergences. Once you have identified a potential turning point using an HPI divergence, switch to short-term oscillators for more precise timing (Section 35).

Answer 129

A. I and III. Prices have rallied above their peak of early May, and HPI rose to a new peak. It shows strong accumulation and indicates that prices are likely to rally higher—go long (Section 35).

Answer 130

C. I, II, and III. Price cycles owe their existence to the fundamental production factors and the mass psychology of consumers and producers, as well as waves of greed and fear among traders. Cycles appear and disappear as market conditions change. Trying to link them to some "immutable laws" including the stars, as some advisors do, is probably an exercise in futility (Section 36).

Answer 131

A. The trend is up, and declines last about half as long as the rallies that precede them. When you want to buy, use short-term oscillators to help identify the exact buying points. You may also buy immediately, depending on how bullish you are. Not buying because it is "too late" means arguing with the trend—not a good trading idea (Section 36).

Answer 132

1. C; 2. D; 3. A, E; 4. B. The season of an indicator is defined by its slope and its position above or below the centerline. When an indicator rises but is below its centerline, it is spring; when it rises above its centerline, it is summer; when it falls from above its centerline, it is autumn; and when it falls below its centerline, it is winter. Spring is the best season for going long, and autumn is the best season for selling short. This chart shows the 1987 stock market crash—the market fell when MACD-Histogram indicated autumn! Seasons are not rigid—not in nature and not in the markets. Notice a brief "Indian summer" in October and a brief "freeze" during early spring (Section 36).

Answer 133

A. Each market timeframe relates to its next greater and lesser timeframes by the factor of 5. When you analyze a market in two timeframes, the shorter of them has to be five times shorter than the longer one. If you want to analyze daily charts, you must first examine weekly charts. No other combination on this list follows the Rule of 5 (Section 36).

Rating Yourself

Fewer than 6 correct	Poor. You need to learn more about the neglected essentials of market analysis. This will give you an edge over most other traders. Please return to the recommended reading materials and retake this test a few days later.
6–11 correct	Below average. You are not in a good position to profit in the markets. Please return to the recommended reading materials and study the essential concepts of time, volume, and open interest.
12–16 correct	Fairly good. You have a working grasp of the essential concepts of technical analysis, which most traders neglect at their peril. Please review your answers to see whether your score was

depressed by a weakness in one area, such as time, volume, or open interest. Then return to the recommended reading list, fill the gaps in your knowledge, and retake this test a few days later.

Over 16 correct   Excellent. You comprehend the ideas that most traders miss. Time, volume, and open interest provide an extra dimension of analysis and deepen your understanding of market dynamics.

Recommended Reading

Elder, Alexander. *Trading for a Living* (New York: John Wiley & Sons, 1993). See Chapter V, "The Neglected Essentials."

Additional Reading

Belveal, L. Dee. *Charting Commodity Market Price Behavior* (1969) (Homewood, IL: Business One Irwin, 1985).

VI

Stock Market Indicators

Answer 134

C. I, II, III, and IV. New High–New Low Index (NH-NL) is a leading indicator of the stock market. It works by measuring daily differences between the strongest and the weakest stocks on any given exchange. New Highs are the stocks that have risen to the highest level in a year and New Lows are the stocks that have fallen to the lowest level in a year on any given day. New Highs are the leaders in strength and New Lows are the leaders in weakness (Section 37).

Answer 135

1. D; 2. C; 3. A; 4. B. When NH-NL rises to a new high for the move, it shows that bullish leadership is growing stronger. It pays to follow the leaders and go long. When NH-NL falls to a new low for the move, it shows that bearish leadership is getting stronger—then it pays to go short. If the broad market rallies but NH-NL traces a lower peak, it shows that the uptrend is losing its leaders and may be in trouble. If the market falls to a new low but NH-NL traces a higher bottom, it shows that the downtrend is losing its leaders and is nearing a bottom (Section 37).

Answer 136

1. E, F; 2. B; 3. A, G; 4. C, D. NH-NL tracks market leaders—it is a leading indicator of the stock market. The market rose slightly higher at B than at A, but there were fewer net New Highs. This bearish divergence gave a sell signal. As the market began to slide, lower bottoms in NH-NL indicated strong bearish leadership. It was a sign to expect lower prices ahead. Stocks fell to new lows in October, but bearish leadership kept shrinking. These bullish divergences gave buy signals. NH-NL confirmed that bulls were in control when it crossed into positive territory (Section 37).

Answer 137

B. II. The market shows a picture-perfect uptrend. Stocks are reaching higher highs and declines stop at higher lows, while NH-NL is rising to new highs for the upmove. This market should be traded only from the long side. This graph reflects stock market activity prior to, during, and after the Iraq/Kuwait conflict in 1990–1991. In July, NH-NL indicated weakness prior to the Iraqi invasion of Kuwait and led stocks down. As the deadline for the allied attack approached and tensions mounted, bullish divergences of NH-NL provided strong buy signals—in the midst of gloom and doom, at the market bottom (Section 37).

Answer 138

C. When the volume of advancing stocks remains disproportionately high relative to their number for several days in a row, it shows that bullishness has reached an extreme point—it has nowhere to turn but down. This sign of an overbought market tells you to go short during bear markets or stand aside during bull markets rather than enter new long positions (Section 38).

Answer 139

C. The same readings of TRIN give different messages under different market conditions. Overbought and oversold readings are higher during bull markets and lower during bear markets. This is why a trader needs to adjust overbought and oversold lines every two or three months (Section 38).

Answer 140

1. A, D, E, F; 2. B, C, G; 3. D–E; 4. B–C. When TRIN reaches a new high or a new low, it shows that the current trend is strong. Buy stocks when TRIN leaves its oversold zone, sell short when it leaves its overbought zone. A divergence between TRIN and a stock market index shows that the trend is weak and ready to reverse. Both divergences on this chart are Class B divergences— not as strong as Class A but better than none (Section 38).

Answer 141

A. Yes, TRIN's latest signal was a sell—but that was a few days ago, and we must decide what to do today. Yes, TRIN is approaching its buy zone—but it is not there yet. An analyst and trader must act in the present time and not dwell on past signals or try to anticipate the future. On the last day of this chart, TRIN is stuck in the midst of its range and does not indicate a clear buying or shorting opportunity (Section 38).

Answer 142

C. I, II, and III. The A/D line measures mass participation in rallies and declines. A rally or a decline is more likely to persist when the A/D line rises to a new high or falls to a new low, in gear with the Dow Jones Industrial Average or S&P 500. Traders need to monitor new peaks and valleys in the A/D line because its absolute level depends simply on its starting date. The A/D line tracks only price changes, not volume (Section 38).

Rating Yourself

Fewer than 5 correct	Poor. If you have no interest in the stock market, then you may skip these indicators. If you plan to trade stocks or stock index futures or options, you owe it to yourself to learn how to use New High–New Low Index and Traders' Index. Please review the recommended literature and retake this test.
5–7 correct	Fairly good. The next time you open your newspaper, you will be able to read the message of new highs and new lows. You may also be able to calculate TRIN and discover whether the stock market is overbought or oversold. Before you proceed to the next chapter, look up the answers to the questions you missed, study the recommended reading materials, and retake this test a few days later.
8–9 correct	Excellent. You understand the essential stock market indicators and know how to use them in trading. If you combine them with advanced computerized indicators (see Chapter 4), you'll be ahead of the market crowd.

Recommended Reading

Elder, Alexander. *Trading for a Living* (New York: John Wiley & Sons, 1993). See Chapter VI, "Stock Market Indicators."

Additional Reading

Arms, Richard W., Jr. *The Arms Index* (Homewood, IL: Business One Irwin, 1988).
Granville, Joseph. *New Strategy of Daily Stock Market Timing for Maximum Profit* (Englewood Cliffs, NJ: Prentice Hall, 1976).

VII

Psychological Indicators

Answer 143

B. I and III. When the majority of traders become bullish, a savvy trader starts selling his positions and looking for shorting opportunities. He knows that bulls are already loaded with stocks, or futures, or options and cannot buy much more. Also, many of them are poorly capitalized—these latecomers are anything but strong and confident. As Humphrey Neill has put it, "When everyone thinks alike, everyone is likely to be wrong" (Section 39).

Answer 144

A. The structure of the futures and options markets ensures that the number of long and short contracts in the same market is always equal. If 75 percent of market participants are bullish, then there are three times more bulls than bears. In that case, an average bear is short three times as many contracts as an average bull is long. In this case, the big money is on the bearish side. Big money did not grow big by being stupid; it pays to bet on the wealthy minority. When bullish consensus rises to 75 percent, start selling and looking for shorting opportunities (Section 39).

Answer 145

D. The number of short and long contracts is always equal. If the majority of market participants are bearish, then the bullish minority must hold more contracts per trader. A 20 percent bullish consensus means that there are four bears for each bull— an average bull holds four times as many contracts long as an average bear is short. With big money on the long side of the market, be prepared for a sharp rally (Section 39).

Answer 146

B. A bull market that has caught the attention of the general public is probably very old and getting ready to reverse. Markets are often very volatile at tops; scaling into a put position may be the safest trading strategy. Trying to buy coffee now means betting on a greater fool theory. Other markets should be traded based on their own merits (Section 39).

Answer 147

A. II; B. IV; C. I; D. III. Traders' positions get reported to the government after their size reaches a reporting level. These levels differ from market to market. Position limits indicate the maximum number of contracts that a speculator is allowed to hold in any given market. Hedgers are exempt from position limits. Many traders are shocked to learn that trading on many kinds of inside information is perfectly legal in the futures markets (Section 40).

Answer 148

A. II; B. III; C. IV; D. I. Commercials deal in commodities in the normal course of business and use futures to hedge business risks. Large speculators are those whose positions reach or exceed reporting levels. If you subtract the holdings of those two groups from open interest, you'll find out how many contracts are held by small traders. The latter group often winds up on the wrong side of market trends. Corporate insiders are officers of publicly traded firms and those who hold 5 percent or more of company shares (Section 40).

Answer 149

D. Buying by corporate insiders is a strong bullish sign. At 11 months, the bear market is old. Nobody will ring a bell to advertise the start of a bull market. As a trader, you may still want to nibble on the short side; but as an investor, it is time to start accumulating the stock you've selected (Section 40).

Rating Yourself

Fewer than 4 correct	Poor. The indicators of mass psychology provide unique insights into the forces that move the markets. It is important to understand how they work, whether you use them in your daily work or not. Please review the recommended reading materials and retake this test.
4–5 correct	Fairly good. You have a decent grasp of the indicators that measure mass market behavior. This may be enough if you only want a general understanding of the concept. If you plan to use them in trading, turn to the recommended reading materials, look up the answers to the questions you missed, and retake this test several days later.
6–7 correct	Excellent. You understand how the indicators of mass market psychology can show whether the market is in a top or a bottom area. Armed with this knowledge, you can use computerized indicators (see Chapter 4) to fine-tune your entry and exit into and out of trades.

Recommended Reading

Elder, Alexander. *Trading for a Living* (New York: John Wiley & Sons, 1993). See Chapter VII, "Psychological Indicators."

Additional Reading

Neill, Humphrey B. *The Art of Contrary Thinking* (1954). (Caldwell, ID: Caxton Printers, 1985).

VIII

New Indicators

Answer 150

A. III; B. I; C. IV; D. II. Each price represents the consensus of value of all market participants at the moment of the trade. Closing prices are especially important because all traders have to live with them until the market reopens. A moving average is an average consensus of value, a composite photograph of prices. The high and the low for each day show how high bulls could lift the market and how low bears could push it (Section 41).

Answer 151

1. D; 2. B; 3. D; 4. A. According to the formula, Bull Power = High – EMA; Bear Power = Low – EMA (Section 41).

Answer 152

C. I, II, and III. Elder-ray shows the power of bulls by measuring how high they can lift prices above the average consensus of value. It shows the power of bears by measuring how deeply they can push prices below the average consensus of value. The exponential moving average, a component of Elder-ray, helps identify market trends. When the trend is up and bears lose power, Elder-ray flags buying opportunities. When the trend is down and bulls begin to slip, Elder-ray flags shorting opportunities. Using Elder-ray, as any other indicator or system, requires judgment; automatic systems do not survive in the markets (Section 41).

Answer 153

1. D; 2. B; 3. C; 4. A. Go long only when the trend is up and sell short only when the trend is down. Do not chase the trend—buy when bears have their feet on the ground. Sell short when bulls have their heads above water. Stay with an uptrend until it reverses or Bull Power shows a bearish divergence, showing that bulls are becoming weak. Stay with a downtrend until it reverses or Bear Power traces a bullish divergence, showing that bears are becoming weak (Section 41).

Answer 154

1. E; 2. D; 3. F; 4. A, B, C. As long as the EMA points down, trade only from the short side. When Bull Power becomes positive during a downtrend, it shows that bulls have come up for air. Wait for Bull Power to tick down (even if it still remains positive) and then place an order to sell short below the low of the last trading day. Cover shorts when a bullish divergence in Bear Power shows that bears are running out of steam. Reverse the procedure in uptrends. As long as EMA rises, trade the market from the long side. Whenever Bear Power becomes negative, it shows that bears have regained their footing. Place an order to buy above the high of the last trading day as soon as Bear Power ticks up (even if it still remains negative). Sell when a bearish divergence in Bull Power shows that bulls are running out of steam (Section 41).

Answer 155

A. The trend is up, and the new peak in Bull Power confirms it. This record peak indicates that the latest price peak is likely to be retested or exceeded. Do not fight the trend and try to pick the top—simply keep ratcheting up your protective stops. Be ready to add to long positions if and when Bear Power turns negative and then ticks up while the EMA still rises (Section 41).

Answer 156

C. I, II, and III. The direction of the move shows whether its force is positive or negative. The distance between today's and yesterday's closing price shows the margin of victory by bulls or bears. High-volume rallies show stronger involvement of the market crowd and are more likely to persist. The greater the distance and higher the volume, the greater the force of the move (Section 42).

Answer 157

D. To calculate the daily Force Index, find the direction and extent of the price change by subtracting yesterday's closing price from today's closing price. Multiply the result by today's volume. Combining these three essential factors allows you to calculate today's Force Index (Section 42).

Answer 158

D. I, II, III, and IV. When the trend is up and the 2-day EMA of Force Index turns negative, it gives a buy signal. When the trend is down and the 2-day EMA of Force Index turns positive, it gives a signal to sell short. Divergences between the 13-day EMA of Force Index and price often mark important trend reversals (Section 42).

Answer 159

1. C, D, K; 2. E, F; 3. A, G, H; 4. B, I. When the 13-day EMA of Force Index rises to a new high, it shows that bulls are very strong and prices are likely to continue to rally. When this indicator falls to a new low, it shows that bears are very strong and lower prices are likely ahead. Bullish and bearish divergences between the 13-day EMA of Force Index and prices mark important turning points in the markets. These signals, while powerful, are not flawless—nothing is ever flawless in the markets. Notice how the bearish divergence D–E got aborted, reminding traders about the need to use stops (Section 42).

Answer 160

B. I and III. The pattern of higher peaks and higher lows means that corn is in an uptrend. The recent new peak in Force Index shows that bulls are strong. Force Index is trending lower, but the distance between its recent peaks is too small to indicate a divergence. The uptrend deserves the benefit of the doubt. It does not pay to guess whether the market is "too high" (Section 42).

Rating Yourself

Fewer than 4 correct	Poor. Take heart—you may not have heard of these new indicators. Please study the recommended reading materials. Whether you plan to use these tools or not, they can show you how to develop your own indicators.
4–6 correct	Below average. You are on the right track, but need to study more. Please return to the recommended reading materials.
7–9 correct	Fairly good. You are starting to grasp new ideas. Please review your answers to see which concepts you've mastered and which require further study. Look up the answers and retake this test in a few days.
Over 9 correct	Excellent. You have mastered the tools known to very few traders. Now you can use them as the building blocks of trading systems (see Chapter 9).

Recommended Reading

Elder, Alexander. *Trading for a Living* (New York: John Wiley & Sons, 1993). See Chapter VIII, "New Indicators."

Additional Reading

Elder, Alexander. *Elder-ray video* (New York: Financial Trading Seminars, Inc., 1990).

IX

Trading Systems

Answer 161

C. I, II, III, and IV. The trend may be up on the daily chart but down on the weekly chart, and vice versa. A trend-following indicator may be giving a buy signal, while an oscillator is giving a sell signal, and vice versa. The Triple Screen trading system is designed to handle these internal contradictions (Section 43).

Answer 162

B. The Triple Screen trading system begins by identifying the trend on a chart one order of magnitude greater than the one you are planning to trade. Find the trend on the weekly chart and then look for entry points in that direction on the dailies. If you begin by analyzing the daily chart and only check the weekly chart later, it is easy to fall prey to wishful thinking. A monthly chart is too far removed from the daily—the timeframes of two charts should relate to one another by a factor of 5 (Section 43).

Answer 163

D. A trader has three choices: buy, sell, or stand aside. The first screen of Triple Screen serves as a censor—it takes away one of those choices. It allows you to trade only in the direction of a trend-following indicator on a long-term chart or stand aside (Section 43).

Answer 164

C. When the first screen of the Triple Screen trading system points up, use declines of a short-term oscillator to find buying opportunities. When the first screen points down, use short-term oscillator rallies to find shorting opportunities. This rule helps you to avoid chasing uptrends and downtrends. In this example, the short-term oscillator is already overbought; wait for its decline before going long (Section 43).

Answer 165

B. When the weekly trend is up and the daily trend is down, Triple Screen points to a buying opportunity. Use its third screen—place a trailing buy-stop above the last day's high to catch a short-term upside breakout (Section 43).

Answer 166

1. A, C, E; 2. B, D, F; 3. B, D, F; 4. A, C, E. When the weekly trend is up, declines of a daily oscillator mark buying opportunities. If the weekly trend is up and the daily oscillator rises above zero, a trader has a choice—to take profits on a long position or to hold. When the weekly trend is down and the daily oscillator rises, it identifies a shorting opportunity. If the weekly trend is down and the daily oscillator falls below zero, a trader may take profits on his short position or continue to hold it (Section 43).

Answer 167

C. III and IV. A bearish divergence is present. It gives a strong sell signal—and a cautious bull would take his profits immediately. Triple Screen does not allow us to sell short when the weekly trend is up, nor does it allow us to buy because the daily oscillator is overbought. When this oscillator declines below zero, it will offer another buying opportunity (Section 43).

Answer 168

1. C; 2. A; 3. B; 4. C. When the weekly trend is up and the daily trend is down, use trailing buy-stops to catch upside breakouts—go long. When the weekly trend is down and the daily trend is up, use trailing sell-stops to catch downside breakouts—go short (Section 43).

Answer 169

C. I, II, and III. The Parabolic system moves its stops in the direction of the trade each day, except that it does not move them into the previous day's range. The faster the trend and the greater the Acceleration Factor, the faster the stops are adjusted. The system works without knowing whether your trade is profitable (Section 44).

Answer 170

C. I, II, and III. Parabolic is especially useful for placing stops during runaway moves, when standard support and resistance zones offer little help. It reacts to the passage of time by moving stops in the direction of the trade and allows you to switch from being long to short, and vice versa. No system, of course, will protect you from yourself. You still have to pick up the phone and place your order (Section 44).

Answer 171

B. The Parabolic system works well in trending markets but leads to whipsaws in trading ranges. Since wheat is in a trading range, simply set your stops using support and resistance levels. Reserve Parabolic for helping you to handle runaway moves (Section 44).

Answer 172

D. I, II, III, and IV. Channels show traders where to expect support or resistance. Channels parallel to trendlines are useful for long-term analysis, especially on the weekly charts. Channels around moving averages are useful for shorter-term analysis, especially on daily and intraday charts. Channels whose width depends on volatility are good for catching early stages of major new trends and for trading options. A few traders use channels whose boundaries are moving averages of the highs and of the lows (Section 45).

Answer 173

C. There is no mystery in constructing a channel. Keep adjusting its width until you find the one that cuts off only approximately 5 percent of the high prices and 5 percent of the low prices. Channels on the daily charts must be based on the price action for the past 2 to 3 months (Section 45).

Answer 174

A. II; B. IV; C. I; D. III. A moving average reflects the average consensus of value. A channel shows the boundaries between normal and abnormal price action. The market is undervalued when it falls below its lower channel line and overvalued when it rises above its upper channel line. The channel coefficients have to be adjusted until a channel contains 90 percent to 95 percent of the price action (Section 45).

Answer 175

C. Amateurs tend to bet on long shots—they buy upside break-outs and sell short downside breakouts. Professionals tend to fade breakouts—selling short as soon as an upside breakout stalls, and buying when a downside breakout stops reaching new lows.

Combining channels with indicators provides the best insights into the power of bulls and bears and helps differentiate true and false breakouts (Section 45).

Answer 176

A. The slope of a channel provides important information to traders. When a channel rises, it shows that the market is bullish; when it falls, the market is bearish; and when it is flat, the market is neutral. A breakout in the direction of the channel slope indicates a powerful trend; a return to the moving average almost always offers a good opportunity to trade in the direction of the trend. Swings between the walls of a flat channel also provide good trading opportunities. Buying and selling at the moving average is not always a good idea. It works when a channel is slanted but not when a channel is flat (Section 45).

Answer 177

1. A, D, F, G, H, I; 2. B, C, J; 3. E. Channels combined with indicator divergences provide some of the best signals in technical analysis. A bullish divergence at the time when prices are hovering at the lower channel line identifies an excellent buying opportunity. Once you go long, place a stop immediately below the latest price low. A bearish divergence at the time when prices are at the upper channel wall points to an excellent shorting opportunity. Once you go short, place a stop immediately above the latest price high. This method allows you to use very tight stops. You can make large profits when it works and lose just a little when it does not (Section 45).

Answer 178

A. This market has to be traded from the long side because its moving average is rising, confirming an uptrend. The recent record peak of MACD-Histogram indicates that prices are likely to retest or exceed their latest price peak. Do not chase the rally, but place a buy order at the moving average and adjust it daily as the moving average rises (Section 45).

Answer 179

C. Bollinger Bands, also known as Standard Deviation Channels, are centered around a moving average. They differ from all other channels because their width keeps changing in response to market volatility. As the market becomes more volatile, its Bollinger Bands grow wider (Section 45).

Answer 180

1. D; 2. C; 3. A; 4. B. Narrow Bollinger Bands indicate low volatility, wide bands high volatility. A breakout from narrow Bollinger Bands often marks a transition from a trading range to a trend. Major trends tend to erupt from flat bases, and it pays to trade in the direction of those breakouts. It pays to buy options inside narrow Bollinger bands where volatility is low and options are relatively cheap. It pays to sell options when the bands are wide, volatility is high and options are expensive (Section 45).

Rating Yourself

Fewer than 6 correct Poor. You do not understand trading systems well. This is dangerous—trading without a system is like sailing without a rudder. Please study the recommended reading materials and retake this test.

6–10 correct Below average. You are starting to catch onto the key concepts, but your knowledge of trading systems is very limited. You need to know a lot more in order to have a chance of success in

	trading. Please reread the recommended reading materials and retake this test.
11–15 correct	Fairly good. You have a working grasp of the essential concepts of trading systems. This level of knowledge may suffice elsewhere but not in dealing with trading systems. You must know them inside out—they help you to survive and prosper in the markets. Please review your answers and look for your weak spots. Then study the recommended reading materials and retake this test a few days later.
Over 15 correct	Excellent. You have mastered the essentials of trading systems. Please review those questions where your answers differed from those given in this book. See whether the discrepancies were due to errors or to your own trading style. Successful traders are creative and can have many differences of opinion. Then proceed to the next highly important topic—risk management (see Chapter 10).

Recommended Reading

Elder, Alexander. *Trading for a Living* (New York: John Wiley & Sons, 1993). See Chapter IX, "Trading Systems."

Additional Reading

Appel, Gerald. *Day-Trading with Gerald Appel* (video). (New York: Financial Trading Seminars, Inc., 1989).

Kaufman, Perry. *The New Commodity Trading Systems and Methods* (New York: John Wiley & Sons, 1987).

Teweles, Richard J., and Frank J. Jones. *The Futures Game,* 2nd edition (New York: McGraw-Hill, 1987).

X

Risk Management

Answer 181

B. Emotional trading is the enemy of success. Greed and fear are bound to destroy any trader who makes decisions based on his feelings rather than intellect. Nobody can get high and make money consistently. A trader can get away with emotional trading for a short while, but is certain to destroy his account. Your goal must be to make the most intelligent trades—not to get elated (Section 46).

Answer 182

C. Most of us like to think that we are smart—and taking losses hurts our egos. Taking a loss means giving up hope that a trade will work out—and nobody likes to live without hope. Good traders are realists; hanging onto a losing trade is not a sound tactic (Section 46).

Answer 183

A. You must believe that you knew what you were doing when you placed your initial stop. You may adjust stops only one way—in the direction of the trade. Giving an unprofitable trade more "breathing room" is a loser's game (Section 46).

Answer 184

C. I, II, III, and IV. The negative mathematical expectation, also known as the house advantage, means that a trader is more likely to lose than to win after taking a series of trades. The positive mathematical expectation, also known as the trader's edge, refers to a series of trades in which a trader is more likely to win than to lose. A trader has to pick and chose his trades very carefully, and take only those that offer him a trader's edge (Section 46).

Answer 185

B. A reluctance to take a loss is a sign of emotional trading. Adding to a losing trade shows that the trader is putting more value into his fantasy of winning than into the reality of a loss. For a loser, a dream is alive as long as he hangs onto his position. But in fact, if you entered a trade on an indicator signal and that indicator has reversed, what's the rationale for staying in that trade? It is not working out—get out and look for a better trade (Section 46).

Answer 186

A. By the time you factor in slippage and commissions, your actual returns are likely to be below the somewhat idealized past record (Section 46).

Answer 187

C. A series of four losses can wipe out trader A, but trader B can hold out until a streak of 40 losses. Trader A is only four throws of the coin away from going bust, while trader B has enough capital to sustain him through 40 unlucky throws. All other factors being equal, the poorer of the two traders will go broke first. This is especially true in trading, because of extra damage from commissions and slippage (Section 47).

Answer 188

B. II, III, I. The first goal of money management is to ensure survival. The second goal is to earn a steady rate of return, and the third goal to earn high returns—but survival comes first. That's how professionals trade; amateurs usually reverse these priorities (Section 47).

Answer 189

A. I. A person who makes a steady 25 percent annual profit is a king of Wall Street. If you can do better than that, more power to you. It is possible to lose over 25 percent in a year and then come back. Risking 25 percent of your equity on a single trade is suicidal. Doubling the size of your trading position involves many factors beyond having a 25 percent profit (Section 47).

Answer 190

B. Never risk more than 2 percent of your account equity on a single trade. This 2 percent rule puts a floor under the amount of damage the market can inflict on your account. The 2 percent rule keeps you out of the riskier trades and protects you from being crippled by a string of losses (Section 47).

Answer 191

B. The 2 percent rule helps you decide how many contracts to trade. Remember, you may not risk more than 2 percent of your equity on any given trade. This means that your maximum risk in a $16,000 account is $320, including slippage and commissions. With a stop $75 away and commission $20, if you buy three contracts, you will still have a small allowance for slippage. Three is the maximum number of contracts you may trade under these conditions. Trading more than that is reckless, trading just one when you see a very attractive trade is counterproductive. Press your advantage when you see a good opportunity (Section 47).

Answer 192

A. If you vary the size of your trades, increase the size of your positions when you are winning and reduce them when losing. In this example, you were savvy enough to reduce your trading size on a losing streak to below 2 percent of your equity. Have the discipline to stick to your plan! Do not blow your advantage now because of a sudden surge of greed (Section 47).

Answer 193

B. If you trade less than the optimal size, your risk decreases arithmetically, while profit potential falls geometrically. This is one of the factors that make trading a hard game. If you risk more than you should, you will go broke, but if you risk less than you should, you will sharply reduce your rate of gain. A greedy person has no patience; he overtrades and busts out (Section 47).

Answer 194

D. I, II, III, and IV. These common money management rules have stood the test of time and also the test of computerized study. Follow these rules; do not break them as most traders do (Section 47).

Answer 195

B. I and II. One of the worst mistakes traders make is to count money while in a trade. Counting money and thinking what it will buy ties their minds in knots, interferes with rational decision making, and leads to losses (Section 48).

Answer 196

A. With a good move under way, you must protect your profits—move your stop to a break-even level or better. You may take profits on one or both contracts if your system tells you that the market is becoming toppy. You are also free to add to your position, as long as your initial position is protected by a stop and the new position does not put more than 2 percent of your equity at risk (Section 48).

Answer 197

A. I. Counting money in a trade flashes a red light—a warning that your emotions are kicking in and you are about to lose money because they will override your intellect. It is a good idea to get out of a trade if you cannot get money off your mind. The time to set profit targets and stop levels and to track your equity is not while you are trading (Section 48).

Answer 198

C. I, II, and III. Stops provide the essential discipline for traders. If you use indicators for finding trades, use them also to get out. You have to extra careful with profit targets—they tend to work better in quiet markets, but trends have a way of outrunning themselves. Grabbing the first profit that comes along is a sure sign of a badly beaten amateur who's lost his confidence (Section 48).

Answer 199

D. I, II, III, and IV. Serious traders place stops the moment they enter a trade and adjust them only one way—in the direction of the trade. When you are long, you may keep your stops in place or raise them but never lower them. When you are short, you may keep your stops in place or lower them but never raise them (Section 48).

Answer 200

A. I. A stop-loss order limits your risk even though it does not always work. Sometimes prices gap through a stop. No stop will protect you from a bad trading system; the best it can do is slow down the damage. A stop is not a perfect tool but it is the best defensive tool we have (Section 48).

Answer 201

D. Break-even orders help protect your equity, but you need to try to minimize whipsaws. This is why it pays to wait for prices to move in your favor by their average daily range for the past few days before moving your protective stop to a break-even level (Section 48).

Answer 202

D. I, II, III, and IV. Make sure to protect some of your paper profits. It is hard to argue with success—when a trade goes in your favor, most methods of protecting profits are beneficial (Section 48).

Answer 203

D. II and III. Review of your actions and self-analysis are essential for becoming a mature, successful trader. You need to study the reasons for entering and exiting trades and pay attention to your feelings while you make trading decisions. You can learn from history (Section 48).

Rating Yourself

Fewer than 7 correct	Poor. The red light is on—you do not understand money management. Before you make another trade with real money, study the recommended reading materials and retake this test.
7–10 correct	Below average. You have a very spotty understanding of money management concepts. Trading with real money at this point is like trying to cross the Pacific in an old boat full of holes. If you continue to trade at your present level of knowledge, your account will sink to the bottom of the ocean. Please study the recommended materials and then retake this test.
11–15 correct	Fairly good. You have grasped the essential concepts of money management. Money management is too important to settle for anything but the top score on this test. Please review your answers to the questions that you answered incorrectly, then study the recommended reading materials and retake this test a few days later.
Over 15 correct	Excellent. You have a working command of the essential money management rules. Please review the questions where your answers differed from those in this book. Money management is a protective wall around your account. Look for every gap in that wall and plug it up.

Recommended Reading

Elder, Alexander. *Trading for a Living* (New York: John Wiley & Sons, 1993). See Chapter X, "Risk Management."

Additional Reading

Balsara, Nauzer J. *Money Management Strategies for Futures Traders* (New York: John Wiley & Sons, 1992).

Vince, Ralph. *Portfolio Management Formulas* (New York: John Wiley & Sons, 1990).

Afterword

Now that you have tested your knowledge of trading using this book, you are better prepared to take the biggest test of all—trading in the markets. Financial trading is a never-ending test of your ability to think straight under stress, make intelligent and unemotional decisions, and stay in control of the money in your account.

This book has given you several rating scales for measuring your skills; it has provided suggested reading lists and has allowed you to retake the tests that you failed at first. Use the same approach when you trade the markets.

The main rating scale of your performance will be the equity in your account. The main sign of getting good marks on your trading tests will be a steady growth of your equity, with small drawdowns. You need to keep track of your equity and stop trading for the rest of the month if it drops more than 6 percent or 8 percent from the highest point reached in the previous month.

For example, two traders may take their accounts from $20,000 to $24,000 in six months, for a 20 percent gain. But compare their performances and decide whether they get identical marks on the market test:

	Trader Jim	Trader John
January	$20,000	$20,000
February	$20,600	$19,600
March	$21,700	$17,300
April	$21,100	$25,800
May	$23,200	$24,100
June	$24,500	$23,200
July	$24,000	$24,000

Who would you rather trust with your money — Trader Jim with his steady gains and small losses or Trader John who has a great knack for losing money but who managed to catch up with Jim in one spectacular month? If you trade like Jim, you are on the right track. If you trade like John, you must stop and think about your trading methods. If your survival depends on an occasional spectacular win, you may not last very long in the markets.

In addition to keeping a chart of your equity, keep a diary of your trades. Whenever you put on a trade, print out the charts and write down your reasons for entering the market. Print an updated chart when you exit that trade and paste it on the opposite page of your diary. Write down your reasons for exiting — perhaps a profit target or a stop was hit, or your system gave you a signal to exit. Write down a few lines analyzing that trade, focusing on what was done right and what could have been done differently. By analyzing your trades you can learn from past experiences and improve your performance.

Discuss your trades with friends — not while you are in a trade but later, after a trade has been closed out. Talking about open positions is dangerous because others may sway you into acting contrary to your own system. Once a trade is closed out, you can benefit from the experiences and opinions of friends you respect.

The fact that you invested the time and energy in studying and taking the tests in this book shows that you are serious about trading. Continue to study the markets, keep your cool, and focus on growing your account equity with minimal drawdowns. Then you will be able to realize your dream — trading for a living.

I wish you success.

New York   Dr. Alexander Elder
November 1992

Sources

Appel, Gerald. *Day-Trading with Gerald Appel* (video) (New York: Financial Trading Seminars, Inc., 1989).

Arms, Richard W., Jr. *The Arms Index* (Homewood, IL: Business One Irwin, 1988).

Balsara, Nauzer J. *Money Management Strategies for Futures Traders* (New York: John Wiley & Sons, 1992).

Belveal, L. Dee. *Charting Commodity Market Price Behavior* (1969) (Homewood, IL: Business One Irwin, 1985).

Douglas, Mark. *The Disciplined Trader* (New York: New York Institute of Finance, 1990).

Edwards, Robert D., and John Magee. *Technical Analysis of Stock Trends* (1948) (New York: New York Institute of Finance, 1992).

Elder, Alexander. *Elder-ray video* (New York: Financial Trading Seminars, Inc., 1990).

_____. *Trading for a Living* (New York: John Wiley & Sons, 1993).

Granville, Joseph. *New Strategy of Daily Stock Market Timing for Maximum Profit* (Englewood Cliffs, NJ: Prentice Hall, 1976).

Kaufman, Perry. *The New Commodity Trading Systems and Methods* (New York: John Wiley & Sons, 1987).

Lefevre, Edwin. *Reminiscences of a Stock Operator* (1923) (Greenville, SC: Traders Press, 1985).

LeBon, Gustave. *The Crowd* (1897) (Atlanta, GA: Cherokee Publishing, 1982).

Mackay, Charles. *Extraordinary Popular Delusions and the Madness of Crowds* (1841) (New York: Crown Publishers, 1980).

Murphy, John J. *Technical Analysis of the Futures Markets* (New York: New York Institute of Finance, 1986).

Neill, Humphrey B. *The Art of Contrary Thinking* (1954) (Caldwell, ID: Caxton Printers, 1985).

Pring, Martin J. *Technical Analysis Explained*, 3rd edition (New York: McGraw-Hill, 1991).

Teweles, Richard J., and Frank J. Jones. *The Futures Game*, 2nd edition (New York: McGraw-Hill, 1987).

Vince, Ralph. *Portfolio Management Formulas* (New York: John Wiley & Sons, 1990).

Index to Questions

ABOUT THE AUTHOR

Alexander Elder, M.D., was born in Leningrad and grew up in Estonia where he entered medical school at the age of 16. At 23, while working as a ship's doctor, he jumped a Soviet ship in Africa and received political asylum in the United States. He continued to work as a psychiatrist in New York City, served as the book editor of *The Psychiatric Times,* and taught at Columbia University. After becoming involved in financial trading, Dr. Elder published dozens of articles, software, and book reviews and spoke at many conferences. In 1988 he founded elder.com, an educational firm for traders. Dr. Elder consults for individuals and financial institutions and conducts seminars for traders. His firm produces videotapes on trading and supplies trading books.

Readers of *Study Guide for Trading for a Living* are welcome to request a current information kit by writing or calling:

elder.com
PO Box 20555, Columbus Circle Station
New York, NY 10023, USA
800-458-0939 or 212-432-7630
Fax 718-639-8889
Email: info@elder.com
Website: www.elder.com